"*Courage after Fire for Parents of Service Members* empowers those of us who are the parents of a returning veteran with vital information and hands-on strategies to better understand and support our sons and daughters after they return home from war-zone deployments. A must-read for every parent of an active duty service member or veteran."

—**Belle Landau**, executive director of Returning Veterans Project and mother of an OIF Veteran

"Whether you're a parent, other family member, or good friend of a service member or veteran who is struggling with readjustment, this much-needed book can help you understand more about what your loved one is going through and show you how you can better assist him or her in coping with the psychological and physical injuries that can result from going to war. Strongly recommended!"

—**Josef I. Ruzek, PhD**, director of the National Center for PTSD Dissemination and Training Division, Veterans Affairs Palo Alto Health Care System, and associate professor, Pacific Graduate School for Psychology

"Written by a remarkable team of mental health professionals with extensive experience in serving veterans and their families, *Courage After Fire for Parents of Service Members* is a treasure trove of information and wisdom for parents of service members returning home from war. Similar to its predecessor, *Courage After Fire,* written for service members themselves, this sequel offers compassionate understanding, critical information, and insights, as well as practical advice for how to survive and even thrive following combat deployment."

—**Douglas K. Snyder, PhD**, professor of clinical psychology at Texas A&M University in College Station and coeditor of *Couple-Based Interventions for Military and Veteran Families: A Practitioner's Guide*

"As a parent of two Operation Enduring Freedom veterans, and as a chaplain who has both served in combat and ministered to thousands of families of combat veterans, I can attest to the need for a guide for parents on how to help their sons and daughters when they return from combat. Parents will greatly benefit from the valuable information in this book. I wish we had this book a decade ago. It fills a huge void."

—**CH (COL) John Morris**, JFHQ Chaplain, Minnesota National Guard and parent of two OEF Veterans

"Domenici, Best, and Armstrong attend to the forgotten family members of our war-fighters—their parents—with compassion, wisdom, and clarity. No matter how old they are or their circumstances, [service members] are someone's children who need help, which this book provides."

—Charles R. Figley, PhD, former USMC SGT, Vietnam Veteran, Tulane University Distinguished Professor, and Kurzweg Chair in Disaster Mental Health

"Fantastic resource! A must-read for every parent with a returning daughter or son. The authors have taken a very complex and critical topic and converted it into an easy reference guide that parents can use to tailor to their family situation. *Courage After Fire for Parents of Service Members* is loaded with insightful suggestions, practical tips, and useful advice that will help parents and service members more successfully navigate their journey together."

—**Alan V. Rogers, Major General, USAF (Ret)**

"*Courage After Fire for Parents of Service Members* gives parents the hope that troubling behaviors and changes will improve over time; it gives them the tools to address their own issues and their service members' issues in constructive, patient ways. I wish my mother had this book when I came home from Vietnam. . . . She would have been less troubled, and I would have been less guilty about how my anxieties hurt her."

—**Anthony Hare, PsyD**, Vietnam Veteran and Executive Director of the Center for Catastrophic Risk Management at the University of California, Berkeley

"At once poignant, enlightening, and instructive for anyone with family or friends in the military! This book is destined to become the authoritative manual for dealing with pre- and post-deployment issues."

—**Nancy Totman**, Blue Star Mom of Navy Submariner

"This beautiful book is a must-read for all parents whose children live and work in harm's way. The authors help parents grasp the wounds war inflicts and the challenges of adjustment after deployment."

—**Sue Johnson, EdD**, professor at Alliant International University and University of Ottawa, Canada, and author of *Hold Me Tight: Seven Conversations for a Lifetime of Love.*

"*Courage after Fire for Parents of Service Members* is the guide every parent must have to cope with the enlistment and deployments of their children, and is something I wish my parents had when I deployed to Afghanistan in 2005. This book shows parents how to do what they have always done throughout their children's lives—take care of them and protect them—especially now, when they need their parents the most."

—**Derek Blumke**, cofounder of Student Veterans of America and Former Director of the Department of Veterans Affairs VITAL Initiative

Courage After Fire *for* Parents of Service Members

Strategies for Coping When Your Son or Daughter Returns from Deployment

Paula Domenici, PhD
Suzanne Best, PhD | Keith Armstrong, LCSW

New Harbinger Publications, Inc.

Publisher's Note

This publication is designed to provide accurate and authoritative information in regard to the subject matter covered. It is sold with the understanding that the publisher is not engaged in rendering psychological, financial, legal, or other professional services. If expert assistance or counseling is needed, the services of a competent professional should be sought.

Distributed in Canada by Raincoast Books

New Harbinger Publications, Inc.
5674 Shattuck Avenue
Oakland, CA 94609
www.newharbinger.com

Cover design by Amy Shoup; Acquired by Melissa Kirk; Edited by Will DeRooy

Library of Congress Cataloging-in-Publication Data

Domenici, Paula.
Courage after fire for parents of service members : strategies for coping when your son or daughter returns from deployment / Paula Domenici, PhD, Suzanne Best, PhD, and Keith Armstrong, LCSW; foreword by Senator Bob Dole.
pages cm
Includes bibliographical references.
ISBN 978-1-60882-715-2 (pbk. : alk. paper) -- ISBN 978-1-60882-716-9 (pdf e-book) -- ISBN 978-1-60882-717-6 (epub) 1. Veterans' families--United States--Handbooks, manuals, etc. 2. Families of military personnel--Handbooks, manuals, etc. 3. Parent and adult child--United States. 4. Veterans--Services for--United States. 5. Veterans--United States--Psychology. 6. Veterans--Mental health--United States. 7. War neuroses--United States. 8. Veteran reintegration--United States. I. Best, Suzanne, 1962- II. Armstrong, Keith (Keith Robert) III. Title.
UB403.D65 2013
355.1'2--dc23

2013014404

Printed in the United States of America

20 19 18

10 9 8 7 6 5 4 3 2

To the parents of our returning veterans:
We thank you for supporting these courageous men and women.

Contents

Foreword by Senator Bob Dole

As a parent, watching a son or daughter deploy to go off to war demands courage and the overriding of a fundamental and powerful instinct: to protect your child from harm at all costs.

Like the men and women who join the Armed Forces and risk their lives in combat, parents largely regard their children's military service with pride, admiration, and love of country. But no matter how much pride and faith we have in our military service members, I have never met a parent who did not feel uneasy or apprehensive about watching their son or daughter go headlong into harm's way.

While military families are some of the most resilient people in America, deployment cycles can be agonizing for those who are safe at home, missing and worrying about their loved ones. Parents are challenged daily when their sons and daughters are overseas. Every lag in e-mail correspondence. Every news report about the war. Every late-night phone call or knock at the door can be stressful.

And then there's the long-awaited reunion. It would be wonderful if all the concerns ended along with the deployment. Some of them do. But more often than not, the concerns do not end when your loved one comes home—the concerns simply change.

Readjusting to civilian life is a deeply personal process that affects the lives of everyone who cares for a returning service member. As a parent, providing care can be tough. A veteran may need support, encouragement, company, or space. Knowing when and how to provide for these needs can be difficult.

In the World War II era, when I completed my military service, the war touched the daily lives of most Americans. The brotherhood and sisterhood of having loved ones in combat was much broader, and the issues were more deeply woven into the everyday lives of all Americans.

Today less than 1 percent of the country's population is serving. And though this generation of service members may feel a general sense of goodwill from their civilian counterparts, their experiences are only vaguely understood by the majority of the country. Most daily lives have not changed during these conflicts.

Useful answers to common questions parents of veterans have are not easily found in movies, newspapers, or television shows. How do you relate to a son or daughter who seems distant since coming home? How do you advocate for a child who is struggling socially, educationally, or vocationally? How do you assist a son or daughter who is experiencing combat stress, especially if he or she is not comfortable asking for or receiving help?

And how do you know when you are nearing your breaking point and need to get help for yourself?

Courage After Fire for Parents of Service Members provides answers to these and other questions. It has been written by an accomplished team of experts on veterans' issues recognized for their first book, *Courage After Fire: Coping Strategies for Troops Returning from Iraq and Afghanistan and Their Families.* Published in 2006, this invaluable book continues to provide support and hope to the families and military personnel affected by the wars in Iraq and Afghanistan.

Now with additional years working with recent veterans and their family members, these three authors are more keenly aware of the unique challenges faced today by parents of service members and have written this second book especially for them. *Courage After Fire for Parents of Service Members* provides insight, guidance, and encouragement to a community of mothers and fathers who are too often overlooked in the public discourse on the needs of our nation's troops.

Being admitted into any branch of the military requires demonstrated achievement, aptitude, and discipline. Children with these qualities are not simply born. They are raised, by parents. You should be as proud of yourself as you are of your son or daughter.

We recognize that many parents like you share the same values of self-sacrifice and commitment to our nation as your military children—you are more comfortable providing support than receiving it. As you read this book, my wife Elizabeth and I hope that you will begin to feel a sense of community—that you are not alone in your struggle to support your son or daughter through post-deployment readjustment. In addition, as you continue to fulfill that fundamental parental instinct of protecting your children and keeping them from harm, we hope that this book will serve as a guide to help you navigate through the ups and downs of this journey.

Your family has been separated by oceans and time zones in the service of our country. There is so much to be learned from your ability to raise remarkable children—to withstand the separations and find success in the challenges of readjustment. All Americans owe you a profound debt of gratitude. Please care for yourself, and know that Elizabeth and I, along with so many of our nation's parents, recognize and honor your courageous contribution to our country.

Thank you and God Bless.

Acknowledgments

We thank the following individuals for contributing significantly to this book by sharing their expertise, knowledge, and editorial comments. Each showed an unwavering commitment to assist us with our goal of writing a much-needed book for parents of service members.

Judy Yarian

Tahle Sendowski, BA

Gerard Choucroun, MSW

Aditya Bhagwat, PhD, ABPP

Additionally, we thank Bridget Leach, LCSW; Lori Daniels, PhD, LCSW; Sherray Holland, PA-C; Candice E. Ortiz, AuD, CCC-A; and Georgina Blasco, AuD, CCC-A, for important contributions to this book. We also want to recognize Ross Burns, LCSW; Judi Cheary; Gary Abrams, MD; John Bosworth, MD; Laura Copland, MA, LCMHC; and Jodi Albert, PhD, for their assistance.

Finally, we thank those generous mothers and fathers of service members who took the time to thoughtfully answer our parent questionnaires, the source of many quotes and testimonials woven into this book. Your honest reflections and accounts of your experiences have been vital to the fabric of this work and offer insights to moms and dads from all walks of life journeying on a path similar to yours. We are grateful to you.

Introduction: To America's Unsung Heroes

Besides watching my son leave on a dingy gray bus to go to war, the hardest thing I have ever had to do is sign a Power of Attorney document for my eighteen-year-old son. (Susan)

Since our nation was founded, millions of US troops have made tremendous sacrifices on behalf of their country. While most Americans go about their daily lives unaffected by the US military presence across the world, you and thousands like you quietly raise and prepare these courageous young men and women for service. You—who bravely wave good-bye as your beloved son or daughter departs for unfamiliar, often dangerous destinations; who endure long separations; and who provide immeasurable care and support before, during, and after deployments—are an unsung hero.

In spite of your significant role and contribution both during and after your service member's deployment, you receive minimal guidance and support. Indeed, we were quite surprised to find that while a few parent testimonials and informal guides exist, this may in fact be the *first* book written by mental health professionals in support of parents like you.

Given our extensive collective experience working with service members and their families, we thank you and every parent like you for the abundant practical and emotional support you provide in the interest of enhancing the health and morale of your sons and daughters who have served. This book is written in honor of your sacrifice and service. May our words provide you with encouragement, comfort, hope, and a sense of community as you help your service member reintegrate after deployment.

You Belong

I knew what I was doing as an adult when I married my Marine. Sending my little boy off to war was a whole new ball game. (Vanessa)

As a parent, you may feel a great deal of pride in your service member for the sacrifices he or she has made for this country, yet helping him or her readjust after deployment can be isolating. Your son or daughter has experienced life-altering events, and you can feel alone or lost as you struggle to relate. And it may feel as if there's a wall separating you from other parents and families in your community because they have no idea what it's like to welcome home someone who served in harm's way.

In our work as mental health professionals, we commonly field questions from worried parents who feel completely in the dark about what to do when they notice changes in their service member following deployment. Whether their service member is visiting, is living nearby, or has moved back home, parents become concerned when they observe unfamiliar behaviors. Eager to reconnect with their service member, these parents often don't know whether to feel hurt, concerned, disappointed, or upset when their daughter refuses to attend family events or doesn't participate in activities or conversations, or when their son seems more interested in playing video games than engaging with family or friends or going to work or school.

He is not the same as when he left. He sometimes [can] be hateful in the way he talks to me. (Charlotte)

Indeed, it can be challenging, or even frightening, if you notice dramatic changes in your service member's personality or behavior. If you spot your service member constantly scanning his or her surroundings while out in public, driving erratically, binge drinking, chain-smoking, or erupting into anger, you may feel alienated and confused. At other times, you may receive shocking news; for example, your daughter didn't tell you that she got married just before she deployed, or your son reenlisted while he was overseas and actually wants to deploy again. Not knowing what to do or whom to turn to for help in these difficult or surprising circumstances, you may be losing sleep, feeling anxious and irritable, having trouble concentrating, or drinking more yourself. At times you may even second-guess yourself and wonder whether you *should* help, concerned that you might interfere with your son or daughter's development toward independence and autonomy. As a result, you may feel frustrated, helpless, and in need of your own support.

In whatever challenging or new circumstance you find yourself after your service member's deployment, understand that you're not alone—there are countless others like you facing similar concerns and challenges. We have written *Courage After Fire for Parents of Service Members* to answer your questions and help you find solutions so you no longer feel lost or alone in your endeavor to understand and care for your son or daughter.

A Bridge to Hope and Understanding

To be honest, the families involved don't get much help, unless children are involved. Or spouses. (Anthony)

Parents of National Guard and Reserves members returning from deployment, or of those separating from the military soon after their return, often describe feeling at a loss as to how to help their son or daughter settle into a civilian routine that now seems much more complex yet less rewarding than life in the military or on active duty. We hear from other mothers and fathers about their disappointment, frustration, or sadness when their service member briefly visits while on leave after finally coming back from deployment but then returns to his or her unit many miles away. For these parents, just when they begin to reconnect with their loved one, they find themselves saying good-bye once again. In addition, when a service member has returned with a physical or psychological injury, like post-traumatic stress, depression, or traumatic brain injury, the task of providing support can be particularly challenging and isolating, especially if the service member refuses to get needed help.

This book will deepen your appreciation of the *military mindset*—a set of survival skills and principles including courage, honor, and self-sacrifice that service members are trained to adopt, yet that doesn't fit with asking for help. Our intent is to complement the tools and skills you already possess to assist you on your post-deployment journey, giving you practical strategies for helping your service member get the support he or she deserves. In this way, we hope *Courage After Fire for Parents of Service Members* is a bridge to hope and understanding.

A Guide to Appreciating Change

> *Yes, my son is different. But part of it is, he is not eighteen anymore and yes, he is a combat vet. There are issues we work through as they reveal themselves and in due time they have and I continue to believe they will, work themselves out. Different doesn't have to be bad—it's just different.* (Monique)

As you understand better than anybody, saying good-bye to your service member not knowing whether he or she will return is a profound experience, and the following months or years of deployment can be an emotional roller-coaster ride. Ultimately, deployment changes your service member. For example, your daughter may have gained greater clarity on what's truly important in life, or your son may have become more responsible after taking on greater roles than were available to him stateside. At the same time, terrible and sometimes unfathomable things can happen during war, and your service member may be struggling with loss or guilt. Deployment also changes *you*, affecting your perspective on life and relationships. During your son or daughter's deployment, you may have been tested like never before, yet discovered just how resilient you are. Your relationship with your son or daughter may have changed—you may have become either closer than you ever imagined or more distant than you expected. In this book, we'll acknowledge various cognitive and emotional shifts that can occur in parents and their service members as a result of the deployment roller-coaster ride and offer you the opportunity to reflect on and address them.

You Matter

> *I'm exhausted from seeing what this has done to my daughter.*
> (William)

As much as you love and wish to support your service member right now, dealing with challenges, unexpected events, and mounting worries and concerns after deployment can be very draining, to say the least. If your service member has returned to live in your home, his or her needs and struggles may at times overwhelm you. Yet it's no easier if your service member has moved far away or has created emotional distance—you may feel exasperated and helpless after several failed attempts at contact. Intensively channeling mental and physical energy into helping your service member with emotional problems, physical injuries, or practical demands can lead to absolute exhaustion. On top of this, you have your own household responsibilities, and in addition you may be caring for children or other family members, not to mention working or participating in other time-consuming activities in your community.

As you focus on your service member's needs while juggling all your other responsibilities, it's easy to forget about taking care of *yourself*. Conversely, any time you do take for yourself may leave you feeling incredibly guilty for placing your needs above your service member's, and so you may no longer enjoy recreational or relaxing activities. This can result in burnout and fatigue, which can have a negative effect not only on you, but also on your entire family. *Courage After Fire for Parents of Service Members* is designed to help you take better care of yourself so that you can better support your son or daughter.

Although we have worked extensively with service members and their families, we have not endured the experience of sending our children off to war and then struggling to assist them after they returned home changed by their experience. We therefore asked mothers and fathers across the country to share with us, in order that we might share with you, their successes and struggles following their son or daughter's deployment. We have woven their heartfelt responses to our questionnaire into this book, in hopes that they will give you a sense of belonging, validation, and inspiration. (For confidentiality we have changed all names and sometimes the gender of the service member or parent, but otherwise, with few exceptions, these are direct quotes.) In many chapters we also illustrate key concepts using one or more vignettes; these are composites based on our clinical work.

About Us

In writing this book, we brought together our combined compassion and experience to assist you in tackling the challenges of supporting your service member after deployment. As mental health professionals, we have worked extensively over the past two decades with active-duty military personnel, members of the National Guard and Reserves, veterans, and their families at military treatment facilities, in Veterans Health Administration (VHA) hospitals, on college campuses, and in private practice offices. We have found it tremendously rewarding to assist our troops and their families in these settings by providing individual, couples, or family therapy and by conducting research to better understand the experience and needs of those who served in war.

In addition, we have advocated for service members and their loved ones by consulting for a wide variety of not-for-profit organizations that support military families, ranging from groups devoted to improving education for children of service members to those that support parents like you. For example, we routinely consult for organizations that provide pro bono mental health services to military personnel and their families, including their spouses, children, parents, and siblings.

Moreover, because we feel strongly about sharing our expertise in this field with students and other mental health professionals, we frequently deliver courses, workshops, and presentations on deployment-related topics both domestically and internationally, and we participate in interviews on issues relating to veterans and their families. Yet with all this collective experience, we agree that our greatest satisfaction to date has been the publication of our first *Courage After Fire* book (Ulysses Press, 2006), a self-help guide for Iraq and Afghanistan veterans and their loved ones. We are gratified to know that our words have reached and helped so many, and we hope that through this new book we can touch the lives of thousands of parents like you.

Overview

With this hope in mind, we begin chapter 1, "Welcome Home! Reintegration Joys and Challenges," by describing the typical needs, priorities, and struggles of service members during the first three years of reintegration. We walk you through the first steps of reuniting with your service member and offer suggestions to assist you through this joyous yet often bumpy period. This chapter addresses common experiences of parents of returning service members, including feelings of neglect or underappreciation, as well as unhealthy habits many service members develop during or after deployment. The aim is to provide you with reassurance and direction following your service member's return.

Building on this understanding, in chapter 2, "Professional, Vocational, and Financial Concerns," we review the demands parents commonly face as they try to guide and support their service member through a host of practical and professional concerns while still fostering his or her independence. We provide tips for helping your service member find a new job, go back to school, or manage his or her finances.

In chapter 3, "Deployment's Toll on the Mind and Spirit: Psychological Injuries and Spiritual Struggles," we move beyond normal readjustment issues to common mental health problems resulting from deployment like post-traumatic stress and depression. After teaching you to recognize signs and symptoms, we offer strategies for assisting your service member to address these problems. In addition, we discuss moral and spiritual struggles, such as guilt and shame, that can significantly affect a returning service member's relationships, work, and overall ability to function.

The goal of chapter 4, "Deployment's Toll on the Body: Physical Injuries," is to review the struggles parents face when caring for a service member who has physical injuries. First, because service members often minimize their injuries, we educate you about signs and symptoms of those less obvious yet more common war-related wounds such as mild traumatic brain injury, physical pain, and tinnitus and equip you with strategies to help. Then, after a brief overview of polytrauma injuries such as amputations and severe traumatic brain injury, we call attention to the emotional toll these serious injuries can have on both you and your service member and offer tips for understanding and managing these reactions.

In chapter 5, "How to Get Your Veteran the Health Care He or She Deserves," we outline the major health care benefits your veteran may be eligible for. This chapter not only reviews important health care options including enrolling in health care through the Veterans Health Administration (VHA) as well as non-VHA services, but also challenges common misconceptions (of parents and veterans alike—particularly younger veterans) regarding VHA services and seeking help in general. A major focus in this chapter is helping your veteran secure good mental health treatment, including advocating for the care he or she deserves.

We understand that supporting and caring for your service member after deployment can affect many of your other relationships and responsibilities. Because of this, we have devoted chapter 6, "Strengthening and Maintaining Relationships within Your Family," to concerns about, or problems you may be having with, your partner (e.g., spouse), your service member's siblings, or your service member's partner. We offer some solutions to common communication problems and include sample scripts to help you initiate uncomfortable and at times painful conversations with family members.

Chapter 7, "Caring Is Wearing: Taking Good Care of Yourself to Better Help Your Service Member," elaborates on the accumulated stress and strain felt by parents supporting or caring for a service member who has readjustment problems or physical or psychological injuries. The focus of this chapter is on ways in which this emotional and physical burden can negatively affect a parent's health and well-being. We present a toolbox filled with strategies for enhancing your self-awareness and self-care to help you manage *compassion stress* and prevent *compassion fatigue* or *secondary traumatic stress* (concepts we explain in this chapter).

Since information is power, there is a list of up-to-date resources at the back of the book, including websites, books, and important phone numbers to assist both you and your service member. Our emphasis is on those sources that offer support services and guidance for parents just like you.

Personalize It

In reading through the overview just now, you probably found that even though many topics piqued your interest and spoke to your struggles, there were some issues that simply did not fit your experience. We encourage you to use *Courage After Fire for Parents of Service Members* in whatever way is most relevant to your unique situation. This may mean reading the whole book from cover to cover, or it may mean selecting only specific chapters of interest. You also may choose to read or share portions of this book with your service member or use it as a companion to our first *Courage After Fire* book.

In this book, the term "service member" is used to refer to all active-duty and discharged US Marines, Navy, Army, Coast Guard, and Air Force personnel, as well as members of the Reserves or National Guard. When we use the word "veterans," we are referring to those who have separated or retired from the military. We use inclusive constructions like "he or she" throughout the book, as well as alternate gender when giving specific examples, to capture the experiences of all the sons and daughters who have served.

We hope that this book is useful not only to parents, but also to anyone who plays an important role in the life of a member of our military who served in harm's way. Although we use the term "parent" throughout this book, our experience has taught us that parental figures come in many shapes and sizes. Whether you are a stepparent, parent-in-law, grandparent, sibling, aunt, uncle, or mentor, the support and care that you provide for your service member is invaluable. We have written this book for you as well.

Finally, we acknowledge and respect that when military sons and daughters are overseas—whether in a war zone, an undeveloped country, or a hazardous landscape—their parents' hearts are with them. This book is for all who have endured that challenge and for those who will rise to meet it in the future. We are grateful for *your* service.

chapter 1

Welcome Home! Reintegration Joys and Challenges

Whether your service member has deployed once, twice, or many times, our goal in this chapter is to help you better understand reintegration and to recognize that it is indeed a process, and a lengthy one. To this end, we'll first provide an overview of what to expect in the first three years of your service member's return so you can begin to acknowledge and address the inevitable changes that come with deployment. This is the first step in helping your service member reintegrate. Next, we'll discuss how to manage reunion and reintegration expectations and disappointments. We'll also provide specific tips for recognizing and addressing unhealthy habits that your service member may be engaging in. Finally, we'll discuss the process of supporting healthy reintegration from both a family and a community perspective.

Year One

> *He can't find a job; is struggling to adjust to life here again. Stuff he experienced while serving in Afghanistan has taken a toll on his emotional stability; he becomes very angry at times over the simplest things.* (Nancy)

Looking back, many service members say that the initial year of reintegration was their most difficult period—and their parents couldn't agree more. While during deployment they yearn for the comforts of home, service members may return to find themselves disoriented and at times quite distressed by what were once familiar surroundings. Seemingly minor changes in their communities, homes, or loved ones are potentially overwhelming to them. You might find yourself having to repeatedly explain to your recently returned son or daughter why you moved the couch to the other side of the living room or changed your hair color by a shade or two. Your daughter may be unexpectedly upset by the closing of a local coffee shop that she rarely frequented, or your son by the death of the neighbor's dog that used to drive him crazy with its barking.

As disorienting as this initial phase of reintegration can be for a returning service member, as a parent you too may feel confused and off balance. If your son or daughter joined the military straight out of high school and deployed soon after, the training, experience, and responsibility of military deployment may have been a "coming of age." For many parents, welcoming home as an "adult" someone they waved good-bye to as a "child" can be quite jarring. Even if your service member's stateside transition has been relatively smooth, you may be startled by the ways in which he or she has changed. These changes may be relatively small—perhaps your daughter who used to take morning walks with you would now rather go for a hard run, or your son no longer enjoys what was once your favorite family TV show. In fact, many of the things that you used to enjoy doing together—going shopping, going to the movies, or driving to the beach—may now be of little interest to your service member. If your service member wasn't living at home prior to deployment, maybe you notice a change in phone or e-mail etiquette: your concerns or questions are met with extremely short, nondescript answers or sometimes no response at all. For some service members, it's simply that their tastes or priorities have changed. For others, having served in a war zone leads them to avoid places where they feel unsafe, such as crowded stores, dark movie theaters, or busy roadways. On the other hand, you may notice a sense of confidence or maturity in your service member that both surprises and pleases you. Military service, including wartime service, can provide tremendous opportunity for personal growth.

Yellow Ribbon Events—for Returning Members of the National Guard or Reserves and Their Families

The Department of Defense (DoD) sponsors Yellow Ribbon* reintegration events approximately thirty, sixty, and ninety days after deployment for those in the National Guard or Reserves (and their family members). These events, organized at the community level, feature local employers, educators, health care professionals, and other service providers, who furnish information about and access to a variety of opportunities and benefits as well as address topics relevant to these returning service members such as how to manage stress, how to manage money, and how to enter the job market.

In the first few months after deployment, your son or daughter may be focused on simply enjoying the comforts of home and the company of family and friends, but we have heard numerous National Guard and Reserve members say that they wished they had taken better advantage of Yellow Ribbon events. Try to attend a Yellow Ribbon event with your service member, if possible. At the event, you can act as reconnaissance, helping your son or daughter gather information and identify resources that will help him or her successfully reintegrate. If someone else (e.g., his or her spouse) accompanies your service member to a Yellow Ribbon event, encourage that person to absorb all the useful information presented at the event.

Currently, not all states provide Yellow Ribbon reintegration programs. Contact your local National Guard Armory for more information.

Note that currently only service members, not families, may attend the 90-day post-deployment events.

**The term "Yellow Ribbon" is also used to refer to a Department of Veterans Affairs (VA) educational assistance program for those discharged from active duty with a service-connected disability.*

Year Two

Fortunately for most service members and their families, the most difficult phase of readjustment is over by the second year. By the second year, you may have come to terms with the ways in which your service member has changed, and you might even have made some adjustments of your own. Perhaps you responded to your service member's complaints and now make the coffee stronger; you no longer drop by unannounced or call first thing in the morning; or you've stopped inviting your service member to large family gatherings. But as much as you've tried to accommodate him or her, you may find that your service member has some lingering bad or unhealthy habits that continue to cause you concern. Maybe you didn't want to "nag" about these habits during those initial months of readjustment, or maybe you just told yourself that they would probably go away. Maybe every time you brought it up you were met with an argument or stony silence. We'll talk more about these problematic behaviors and how to address them later in this chapter.

While for the majority of service members, the first year of reintegration poses the most challenges, it's generally the second year in which we begin to see the real cost of wartime deployment. By the second year, you may begin to see signs of psychological injuries, such as those we'll discuss in chapter 3. Some service members experience a delayed reaction to the stress of deployment or gradually find themselves overwhelmed by the pressures of reintegration. Others who successfully hid their injuries at first are no longer able to maintain their cover. For some, the end of a relationship or loss of a job is the final straw that sends them spiraling into depression.

As you know, a parent's hearing is naturally attuned to the sounds of his or her own children. You may recall being able to hear "Mom!" from across a crowded playground and know with certainty that it was your child who was calling. Or awakening in the middle of the night to your child's cough or dream-state whimper. Because you may be better able than anyone else to hear your service member's subtle cries for help, it's important that you continue to listen—and watch—for signs and symptoms of psychological injury through this pivotal year of reintegration.

Year Three

By the third year, your service member may be dealing with the last vestiges of the reintegration process. For many service members, by this time issues that arose during the first year have smoothed out, and though they might think about some aspect of their deployment nearly every day, they are firmly planted in their present lives and communities, and often their outlook is more hopeful. But for some, injuries suffered during deployment have festered, becoming chronic conditions. Those who have sought treatment may be starting to experience some relief, while others may be just now coming to terms with the fact that their injuries will not heal on their own. If your service member is still struggling to readjust and has signs or symptoms of psychological injury (see chapter 3), *it's never too late to heal.* While the path to healing is generally shorter and easier for those who seek help early on, both you and your service member have every reason to believe that recovery is possible and within reach.

Multiple Deployments

Each deployment changes her. She still loves her family, but in a more distant way. (Christophe)

We recognize that many parents have watched their service member deploy two, three, four, or even more times before having the opportunity to fully reintegrate. You may have seen your daughter deploy while still struggling to readjust from an earlier deployment, or you may have waved good-bye to your son knowing that he had psychological or physical injuries from which he had not yet recovered. Unfortunately, in recent times, multiple deployments have become the norm and taken a heavy toll on our nation's troops. At the very least, just knowing the likelihood of future deployments may have caused your service member anxiety, impeding his or her readjustment and recovery. It's also true that stress and injuries can be cumulative over multiple deployments, and psychological wounds suffered during an initial deployment may deepen as a result of subsequent war-zone service.

Still, when called upon, many service members eagerly deploy again—proud to serve their country and to support their unit—and return in essentially the same condition as before. Others, however, dread yet another deployment as they struggle to heal from psychological injuries. Still others show significant signs of injury but surprisingly want to deploy again rather than seek treatment (or "re-up" rather than transition to civilian life). When this happens, it's sometimes the injury itself that drives service members to return to the "safety" of the war zone, where they are no longer faced with the struggles of readjustment and the stressors of stateside expectations, responsibilities, and relationships.

If you are concerned that your service member has suffered psychological injuries that will be exacerbated by another deployment—even if he or she is already scheduled to deploy—it's important that you speak with him or her directly. Begin the conversation with something like **"I'm wondering whether you may be deploying again before you have had a chance to recover from your last deployment."** One way to describe the problem is in physical terms: it's as if your service member had suffered a back injury and is deploying again before it has fully healed. If your service member is currently receiving psychological treatment, suggest that he or she ask a military mental health provider about the safety and appropriateness of deploying. Although your service member may very well still have to deploy, it can be helpful for him or her to speak with a provider about ways to try to mitigate a surge in symptoms or to curtail further injury. If your service member is *not* in treatment and you have concerns, suggest that he or she speak to a provider anyway. Providers at military treatment facilities should be familiar with the most current regulations about deployment-limiting conditions, such as circumstances or medications that could affect a scheduled deployment.

The Reintegration Roller-Coaster Ride

> *For his first homecoming…we were able to see each other for 15 minutes standing in the driveway of our home. I hugged him and remained calm because I did not know what to do or say and I did not want to seem weak in his eyes.* (Colleen)

Parents eagerly and even anxiously awaiting their service member's return often envision a reunion filled with ceremony, fanfare, and joyful gatherings. Many feel a mixture of excitement, pride, and relief upon seeing their service member home safe, and later they may fondly remember the various activities and events that filled the following weeks and months. It's not unusual for parents to go to great lengths to prepare favorite meals or otherwise ensure their service member enjoys all the comforts of home.

If you are currently awaiting your service member's return, similar thoughts of reunion and attending to your son or daughter's needs may occupy your mind. As a parent, you may be used to putting your child's needs and wishes above your own, but as we have learned, post-deployment reintegration is not just a service member's struggle. It presents challenges the whole family must face, both individually and together.

You may find, for instance, that after deployment, your once considerate and helpful daughter seems suddenly self-focused and unappreciative. She may appear to have no interest in anything other than fulfilling her own basic needs of good sleep, good food, and hot showers, each of which she partakes of in abundance. Or maybe your son is focused on simply "having fun" in any way possible and is disinterested in attending anything "serious" or "boring" like church services or family gatherings. Even the simple activities that you used to enjoy together may no longer appeal to this seemingly different person. After all those agonizing months in which you dreamed of his or her safe return, it's understandable that you would feel disappointed, unappreciated, or just plain hurt by this kind of attitude and behavior. Rather than feeling guilty for having these thoughts and emotions, acknowledge that reintegration is a process that affects each member of the family, including you.

Deepening Your Understanding

He wolfed down his food. Didn't flush the toilet! His room was a mess and he left wet towels on his bed. He didn't call when he was going to be late getting home or if we were out didn't leave a note where he was. If he was hungry, he ate even if I was fixing dinner at the time. Do I like that?...no. Is it the end of the world? no. Does it get better with time? yes. (Jessica)

One way that you can ease the reintegration process is by deepening your understanding of what is driving your service member's behaviors. For instance, while as a parent you may find gratification in providing your son with the comforts of home, his sometimes seemingly insatiable need for certain foods or activities may appear to you unreasonable, lazy, or even reckless. When considering the impact of deployment, don't underestimate the level of deprivation and discomfort that your service member may have experienced. Because within the military culture, those who complain are seen as weak or "whiners," it's likely that your service member will never share with you the full extent of what he or she had to endure—sleeping on an uncomfortable cot, continually awakened by mortar fire or explosions; carrying heavy equipment over harsh terrain through even harsher weather; surviving on MREs (Meals Ready to Eat: there's a reason why these precooked packaged meals can survive for years under any condition); inadequate or nonexistent toilet or hygiene facilities with all the associated odors and potential health issues; or all of the above.

Freedom

Be flexible and open. If they have a "To Do" list, offer to help with that....get a shower curtain, towels, whatever. Give them a safe haven but also alone time. Recognize that they need time to decompress. (Joshua)

While deprivation and discomfort can make the simplest of stateside comforts seem a luxury, what some deployed service members miss the most is their freedom: freedom to hop in the car and go to the movies; to hang out with friends and party till dawn; or to drink, eat, and wear whatever they please. Some may simply miss the freedom to say no—"No, I don't want to go to Uncle John's"; "No, I'm not getting up now"; or "No, I don't feel like mowing the lawn." After months and months of following orders, some service members become downright defiant once they're home, simply because they can. Still others express their independence through avoidance. They "disappear" just before relatives arrive, sleep their way through meals, or become "too busy" to respond to phone calls.

Dos and Don'ts

In contrast to seeming less motivated, you may find that your formerly laid-back, relaxed son or daughter has been transformed into a rigid, rule-driven person. This can be particularly true of anyone who served in a position of rank with responsibility for the supervision and safety of troops. Maybe you've found yourself being lectured on how to drive or how to make your bed. Maybe your daughter now has a long list of dos and don'ts that you and your entire household are expected to adhere to. Or maybe your son has established a strict schedule of activities that can't be deviated from for any reason.

Having to adjust from a rule-bound, efficient military environment to the seemingly undisciplined, unstructured civilian way of life can be quite frustrating. You may find, for instance, that your service member has no patience for inefficiency: the grocery-store clerk is too slow and sloppy, the dry cleaner can't seem to press anything right, or civilian coworkers are lazy and irresponsible. In addition, those who have deployed are often intolerant of the "petty" complaints of friends and family members. You may be chastised for complaining about the weather or that you don't know what to buy. Even things that you think are justifiably upsetting—a broken air conditioner, a lost wallet, a rained-out event—may be trivial and meaningless to your service member relative to the destruction and loss of life that he or she has witnessed. For some who have deployed, if it's not life threatening, it's not important.

The Search for Meaning or Purpose

> *There is also an adjustment to having a family member return and integrate back into family life. You need to realize that the person who depended on your letters and care packages for months is now back independent and ready to go his way—like it or not!* (Andria)

Some service members have a difficult time finding meaning or purpose in much of anything after deployment. The level of responsibility and sense of mission that they had during deployment is difficult to find in civilian or even active-duty military positions stateside, and they may feel a lack of respect or dignity in their current employment.

The search for meaning and purpose can be especially difficult for those who entered the military straight out of high school or at a very young age. Even under normal conditions, adolescents struggle to answer fundamental questions such as "Who am I?" and "What's it all for?" as they develop into young adults. When asked within the context of war, these questions can be utterly overwhelming. As a parent, you may feel overwhelmed as well by the recognition that your child is now truly an adult who must deal with these issues. We'll say more about such struggles in chapter 3.

Regardless of exactly how your service member has changed, reintegration challenges can cause you to feel disconnected from him or her in ways that you hadn't anticipated as you eagerly prepared for his or her homecoming. Watching a person you thought you knew behave in unrecognizable ways can be disconcerting as well as disorienting. But keep in mind that your service member may be equally confused and destabilized by these changes. If you are having difficulty connecting with your service member, the odds are good that others are as well. Maybe your daughter is having trouble relating to the civilian world in general. Or maybe your son is simply overwhelmed by demands placed on him by family, friends, and stateside responsibilities, while at the same time being pulled toward the buddies he served with and by a continued sense of loyalty to the mission.

Supporting the Process

> *We have found that just letting her be in her room by herself for a couple of hours is a treat for her. We found that allowing her some down time really perks her up. They are rarely alone while they are deployed.* (Fernanda)

There are ways in which you can ease your service member's struggles while at the same time supporting your own process of adjustment. To begin with, it's important that you evaluate your expectations for your service member and consider whether and to what extent they are reasonable and appropriate.

Managing Expectations

You may, for instance, continue to expect your daughter to attend Sunday dinner, to call at least once a week, or to join family trips just as she had always done prior to deployment. When she fails to meet these expectations, you may feel hurt and rejected. Rather than redouble your efforts to cajole your service member into attending family functions, first consider some of the issues mentioned above as potential explanations for your service member's behavior. Next, make a list of your expectations and decide which ones should be firm, which ones can be flexible, and which ones you are willing to set aside for now or even permanently. Then, find a time to sit down with your service member and calmly ask about his or her thoughts and feelings regarding your expectations. What does he or she see as reasonable and appropriate and why? What does he or she see as unnecessary, uncomfortable, or even overwhelming? You may be surprised. Maybe your son feels so alienated or "different" from his nonmilitary cousins that he is uncomfortable attending family functions. Or maybe your constant questioning about deployment experiences has caused your daughter to feel anxious and overwhelmed, leading her to avoid conversations with you about anything. Maybe family trips now only serve as a painful reminder of wartime service. While in some instances you may be able to mitigate the situation, you may agree that other expectations are indeed no longer important.

Building Communication

[We were on] the patio one night, listening to some of his music, while we had a few drinks, smoking cigars, listening to tales of his deployment. In a relaxed mode, on his own terms, he opened up and told us his year-long experiences one by one—the good, the not so good, and the downright ugly. It was helpful to him and eased our minds.
(Mark)

Discussing expectations is one way to fortify the lines of communication between you and your service member in support of the family reintegration process. Many parents go to great lengths to maintain regular and positive communication with their service member during deployment, but it's equally if not more important to keep communication channels open during the reintegration process. Helping your service member feel safe to share what is really on his or her mind, without judgment, will promote successful reintegration. However, if your service member thinks that every conversation will involve some type of criticism of his or her behavior, his or her comrades, or the military in general, he or she may return to a "fight-or-flight" deployment skill set and either argue with you (fight) or avoid talking with you (flight).

One of the best tools for transitioning between deployment and post-deployment communications is the sharing of photos, videos, and other memorabilia that tell the story both of your service member's deployment and of your experience and your family's experience while he or she was away. While you and your service member may have exchanged photos or video streams over the Internet during deployment, this cannot compare to sitting down and sharing these memories and experiences face-to-face. In addition to strengthening your relationship and communication, you will be helping your service member create a coherent story of his or her deployment, which makes reintegration easier. If you can share milestones or describe certain events that occurred in your service member's absence, he or she will feel less like an outsider.

You may find it helpful to let the conversation unfold over a couple discussions rather than trying to cover everything all at once. The value of this exchange cannot be overstated. However, as the communication channels deepen, it's possible that your service member will share some unexpected or disturbing news. You may hear, for instance, about injuries, traumas, or losses; about intimate relationships or sexual harassment; or about alcohol or drug use or disciplinary actions; or you may hear unsettling news about your service member's discharge status. Because during these moments—some of which may feel like confessions—your service member may blurt things out in a rush of emotion, it's natural that you might respond with equal distress and anxiety. It's important, however, to withhold judgment and reserve comment as much as possible until you have had the opportunity to process the information and sort through your own feelings. In the meantime, a simple hug and a few general words of support may be best. The power of listening, "reflecting" (saying back or paraphrasing what the other person has said, to indicate you heard and understand), validation, and empathy can go a long way toward building a safe connection. This does not mean that you must hide your emotions entirely; there are many situations in which tears are an appropriate, compassionate response. But it's also appropriate to let your service member know that you need some time to digest the news before discussing it further. Although your service member may want to discuss his or her experience on his or her own terms, you may need to point out that spewing it all out at once is not necessarily the best approach for either one of you.

Unhealthy Habits

Bruce had deployed twice, and the sense of responsibility and thrill of leading his platoon members and keeping them safe was something he couldn't match back in Jacksonville, North Carolina. Although he loved his wife and his two-year-old son, he wanted to go back on deployment as soon as he could. But he wasn't due to deploy again for a while. So he took to riding his motorcycle, fast, for three to four hours a day—whenever he could—even when his wife pleaded for him not to. As she worried for his safety, he rode to escape the pressure of family life, for the thrill and "high," and to avoid everyone around him who couldn't understand what he'd been through. What else could he do?

Other issues or problems may have carried over into the reintegration period. If your service member lives with you or if you see each other often, you may have noticed excessive smoking, excessive Internet use, excessive gambling, or other obsessive, addictive, or unhealthy behaviors. If you do not witness such problem behaviors firsthand, you may hear about them from others: for example, you may learn from your daughter-in-law that your son is struggling with alcohol or is taking unnecessary risks for the "high" like Bruce.

You may not know how to address these behaviors or even whether you should.

What exactly is an "unhealthy" or "bad" habit? It's a tendency to repeatedly engage in a pattern of behaviors that negatively affects a person's physical or psychological health, usually associated with poor self-control (Segen's *Concise Dictionary of Modern Medicine*, s.v. "bad habit"). Often, individuals use these behaviors to cope with or avoid negative feelings, such as anxiousness, emptiness, or even boredom. Consider cigarette smoking: People commonly smoke to calm their nerves or feel more relaxed. It serves as a temporary escape from stress. Some individuals don't consciously know why they began engaging in a bad habit; however, it can gradually take over and become something they just can't shake.

If your service member is currently showing signs of engaging in an unhealthy habit, it's possible that this behavior developed during deployment, where it may have served a useful or positive function, like constant scanning to detect threats in the environment (see below). After deployment, however, such behaviors may cease to be helpful and can interfere with the ability to fully reintegrate. Alternatively, the habit you are concerned about may be one that existed before deployment but has worsened since your service member returned, or it may be totally new. Keeping these points in mind, let's review common unhealthy habits of service members after deployment, and then we'll discuss how you might help as a parent.

Obsessed with Deployment News

After deployment, some service members become preoccupied with following the latest deployment news, spending endless hours tracking what's going on with their unit and comrades or what's happening in the area of operations where they were deployed. The desire to keep up with this news is normal to some degree, but for many individuals, the drive takes on a mission of its own. It's as if they're back on deployment as their obsession to find updated information—on the Internet (e.g., on social networking sites), in the newspaper, and on TV—overshadows their ability to live in the present and thus impedes their readjustment to stateside or civilian life.

Glued to High-Tech Gadgets

It's not uncommon for service members, especially younger ones, to become addicted to surfing the web, checking Facebook, e-mailing, playing video games, or engaging in other stimulating activities on devices like smart phones or tablets. In addition, they may enjoy playing violent video games or watching war scenes because it triggers the same "high" or adrenaline rush they felt while serving in a danger zone. These engrossing activities can become an incredibly hard habit to break. One downside of spending long periods of time alone glued to a screen is that it can replace in-person interactions with friends and family or participation in other activities, with the result that loved ones, including you, may feel neglected or disregarded.

Driving Fast

High-speed driving or motorcycle riding is another thrill-seeking habit we frequently hear about. Since aggressive driving is regarded as an essential war strategy and even a lifesaving tactic in certain theaters of operation, it's not unusual for service members to engage in this activity when they first return to driving or riding their motorcycle in the states. However, some continue this high-risk behavior even after they've been home awhile—they use it to escape boredom in pursuit of that adrenaline rush or thrill, as in Bruce's case. This reckless behavior becomes addictive, despite the potential harm or even loss of life.

Always on Guard

Being constantly on high alert is useful to service members in detecting and responding to threats while deployed. But when this hypervigilance or "situational awareness" is practiced stateside, it can evolve into a bad habit that not only interferes with service members' ability to enjoy realistically safe places and activities, but also depletes them of substantial amounts of emotional and physical energy because it takes so much effort to be constantly scanning one's environment.

During deployment, many service members learn to either be prepared for danger when entering crowded, loud, or dark places or avoid these situations altogether. After deployment, some end up avoiding similar places and situations because they're afraid they won't be able to protect themselves or their loved ones or that something bad or dangerous will happen. Yet when they routinely avoid going to shopping malls, restaurants, or even movie theaters because these places feel unsafe or out of control, their lives as well as the lives of their loved ones can become seriously constricted.

Gambling Galore

Another bad habit fairly common among service members after deployment is gambling. Although it's certainly not unusual to gamble here and there—for example, to play poker, buy lotto tickets, go to a casino, or bet online—when this activity becomes compulsive, it obviously has negative consequences. This risky behavior can steal a person's attention away from important professional, personal, and family responsibilities and lead to serious financial problems. In addition, secrecy, lying, and even stealing to hide a gambling habit can cause significant family conflict.

Defensive Tactics: Pornography and Serial Affairs

Regularly viewing pornography or going to strip clubs is another risky habit that some service members adopt. Like high-speed driving, this thrill-seeking behavior is often employed as a means to find that excitement missed from deployment days. It also can be an escape from the realities of romantic obligations or commitments, or a retreat into a fantasy land that, for the short term, distracts from the pressure of real-life relationships. While such behavior may initially seem like "no big deal" to the service member, its eventual consequences can be irrevocable (e.g., breakups, divorce, impaired performance of work and household responsibilities).

In addition, it's not uncommon for service members to engage in serial affairs after deployment, which can become a way not only to satisfy sexual urges or needs but also to avoid intimate, monogamous relationships. Following deployment, some service members' views shift: for example, they see close relationships as dangerous because the thought of losing or being rejected by a partner is extremely painful. Thus, for these individuals, serial affairs, as well as use of porn, become a defensive maneuver—a way to protect themselves from experiencing deeper, more vulnerable emotions.

Cigarette Smoking

One of the most common habits we notice among service members after deployment is cigarette smoking. Some service members take up smoking while deployed; others who previously smoked in moderation may now smoke continuously. While some find smoking calms them during periods of stress, others smoke when bored or as a way to occupy themselves when they are feeling fidgety. Still others find smoking a good excuse for taking a break from work or social gatherings. Even though the health consequences of smoking are well known, many people smoke anyway, and the habit is awfully hard to kick.

Drinking and Using Substances

> *He has a hard time sleeping, he drinks and passes [out] to ease the nightmares.* (Stephanie)

Use of alcohol, illicit substances such as marijuana, or substances like "spice" (synthetic cannabis) as a "quick fix" to numb or block out negative feelings such as anxiety, boredom, grief or even nightmares is very common among service members after deployment. A similar habit can develop involving prescription drugs such as painkillers, stimulants, or antianxiety medication. Easy and legal access to alcohol, and increased availability of certain illegal or prescription drugs, may help fuel the fire, leading service members to look to these substances for short-term relief from their problems or to help them have fun or socialize. However, such substance use can have long-term serious physical and psychological repercussions, including dependence.

While caffeinated drinks like coffee and soda as well as energy drinks like Red Bull and BOOST can temporarily help individuals in a deployed setting fight fatigue and stay vigilant in order to do their jobs effectively, they can also become addictive. Constant consumption of these drinks in order to feel amped or energized after deployment is a bad habit.

Supporting Change

If you're wondering whether you should talk to your service member about any of the behaviors described above, or others that seem unhealthy, answering the questions below can help you decide. If you don't know the answers, talk with others who are close with your service member to gather as much information as possible. You may not be able to get all the information you're looking for, but with the help of friends and family you should be able to compile a good snapshot of your service member's behaviors.

- How often does the behavior occur? (e.g., every day, weekends only, a few times a week)
- How long does the behavior last each time? (e.g., a few minutes, an hour, several hours)
- Is this a change from previous behavior?

    - Did your service member practice this behavior before deployment? If yes, how often? How does that compare to now?
    - Did your service member practice this behavior during deployment? If yes, when did it start and how often did it occur?
    - Is this behavior completely new? If yes, when did it start and how often does it occur?
    - How has this behavior developed over the past few months—has it worsened, stayed the same, or improved?

- Have you asked your service member the reason for this behavior? If yes, how was it explained? If no, what might happen if you asked this question?

- How is this behavior affecting your service member and his or her reintegration? Consider the following areas:
    - Work/school (e.g., concentration, focus, performance, deadlines, attendance)
    - Physical health (e.g., sleep, stamina, exercise, weight, pain)
    - Mental health (e.g., mood, attitude, motivation, energy level)
    - Loved ones (e.g., you, other family members, partner, children, friends)
    - Household responsibilities (e.g., chores, finances, upkeep)
    - Personal goals/interests (e.g., hobbies, aspirations)

This should help you see objectively whether there is good reason to believe that your service member's habit is risky and/or harmful. Remember, the behaviors we have discussed typically begin as coping strategies, but when your service member uses them habitually, showing little self-control and despite negative consequences for his or her health and well-being, they have turned into problems that need to be addressed.

If you think your service member's pattern of behavior has turned into an unhealthy or potentially harmful habit, consider using the sample script below to talk to him or her about your concerns or sharing it with someone you trust (e.g., your spouse) who could broach these sensitive issues with him or her. Or you can write your own script, using the one below as a guide. Rehearse the script beforehand, and remember to be nonjudgmental, empathic, and a good listener when you actually raise the topic. This will help prevent your service member from becoming defensive or withdrawn.

"I've noticed/heard since you got home that you're ________________ (name the unhealthy behavior: e.g., smoking, drinking, playing computer games) more than before you left. You may not pick up on the amount of time/energy/money you're investing in this behavior since it seems as if it has almost become a habit for you—something you're used to doing without thinking about it. I'm worried that this habit may be negatively affecting your ______________ (be specific: e.g., performance at work, ability to concentrate, sleep, ability to socialize with family). I'd like to talk to you more about this because I want the best for you and your health."

How to Kick Unhealthy Habits

Once you've had a conversation with your service member about the behavior that concerns you, or someone else has opened the door to this topic, encourage your service member to take the following five steps to become more aware of the unhealthy habit and strategies to overcome it:

1. For two weeks—using a notebook, smart phone, tablet, calendar, or whatever is convenient—track the amount of time spent on the habit.

Just as he or she might track time spent doing certain exercises at the gym, this will allow your service member to see just how much time and energy he or she is devoting to the habit, which may help create motivation for change.

2. During this same two-week period, monitor thoughts, feelings, and body sensations both directly before engaging in the habit and afterward.

   Once your service member has gathered this information for two weeks, have him or her look for patterns—that is, what he or she is typically thinking and feeling immediately before and after practicing the habit. For example, your son may notice that when he's feeling anxious or has muscle tension, he drinks. After he drinks, he feels more relaxed and less tense.

3. Brainstorm (with you or a trusted other) healthy strategies to deal with the thoughts, feelings, and sensations identified through this self-monitoring process.

   Jot down ideas; be creative and open-minded.

4. Weigh (with you or a trusted other) the pros and cons of the habit.

   Together, consider the short- and long-term advantages and disadvantages, including the impact on relationships, military/work/school responsibilities, physical and mental health, and overall functioning. Determine whether there is enough motivation for change. If there is, choose one or two practical replacement strategies identified in step 3 to "check out" and use during the next two weeks in lieu of the unhealthy habit.

   If your service member doesn't want to change, continue to collaboratively discuss with him or her the role of this habit in his or her life. Be curious and nonjudgmental. If you're not the right person to do this, invite somebody else your service member trusts (e.g., his or her partner) to have this discussion.

5. Speak with a friend, a family member, somebody from the military, or a community figure—any role model—who can share the experience of having "kicked" a bad habit. Or read a book or watch a documentary about an admired person (e.g., athlete, military hero, actor, politician) who overcame a bad habit and represents a success story.

Don't Forget the *Healthy* Habits

The military promotes many healthy habits and positive behaviors that can be leveraged to help your service member reintegrate and kick unhealthy habits. One strategy you can use to help your service member beat an unhealthy habit is to highlight military values such as the following:

- Working as a team player
- Commitment to the mission
- Self-sacrifice and giving back to society
- Hard work and discipline
- Integrity and loyalty
- Regular exercise and staying physically fit
- Building strength through adversity

Help your service member identify what he or she has gained from adopting positive behaviors in line with these values—maybe a sense of achievement, respect from others, a job promotion, or good physical health. Your service member may never have thought about the things he or she did in the military as healthy habits, when indeed those practices serve as excellent examples of self-improvement and self-care. Juxtapose these with the unhealthy habit you're concerned about and ask your service member to identify its negative consequences—maybe lack of direction, isolation from loved ones, poor job performance, or poor physical health. Remind your service member that he or she is capable of adopting or strengthening healthy habits that can replace unhealthy ones, and brainstorm what the advantages are. Then help your service member jump-start those healthy habits stashed in his or her rucksack or incorporate those already in use more fully into his or her life.

Too Much of a Good Thing

Don't forget to remind your service member that even healthy habits can have a dark side if they are too rigidly adhered to. Running on an injured leg, for example, can lead to more serious physical problems. Working too much—to the exclusion of other aspects of life—can also lead to difficulties. Moderation is the key, even when a habit is healthy!

Reintegration—It's a Community Process

Up to this point, we have not focused much on the role of community in the reintegration process. Be aware, however, that reintegration into the community can run the gamut from being smooth and positive to being extremely difficult. If your service member is transitioning to a military base, he or she is returning to a community that is typically sensitive to what it's like to "come home." Military personnel and families living on or near the base may be unified in their efforts to welcome home loved ones and fellow service members when rotations return. Some members of the National Guard or Reserves utilize their once-a-month obligation as a time to reconnect with other service members who understand what they are going through in their transition back to the community.

At the same time, some individuals returning from a deployment don't come home with their unit; they may have been deployed to the theater of operations as an individual augmentee (without anyone else from their unit or maybe even their home base), so when they return to base, they can feel like an outsider among other service members.

Communities not located near military bases, particularly those with few service members, may be much less sensitive or simply oblivious to the experiences of troops returning from deployment. Even though some in these communities may be interested in supporting returning service members, they may not know how to address their needs or how to forge connections with them. While some community members will make an effort to welcome your service member home, others won't know how to interact with or respond to him or her (or even see the need). For example, someone may ask your daughter how her deployment was, but react poorly, leaving her wary of talking about her military service and less likely to participate in community activities or events. In addition to being awkward for your service member, this may be hard for you to watch or hear about.

Some civilians have numerous preconceived notions about service members. Even other parents of service members may respond in an insensitive manner about an issue with which your family is struggling. While some people can (and should) be educated about military service, others may simply be incapable of understanding. It's probably better to avoid discussing issues such as deployment and reintegration with those who are not interested in learning about the military experience and instead relate to them on other, more familiar topics or activities.

At the same time, it's not only the community that has a role here—your service member may need to play catch-up with the civilian world. He or she may need to work to fit in by participating in community events and showing interest in the things and people around him or her. This may mean joining a church or a temple, becoming active in local politics, joining a book club or other leisure interest group, or volunteering for a community project. It could mean becoming a Little League coach, volunteering with a local veterans group, or working at a soup kitchen. Unfortunately, some service members won't be interested in participating in community activities; others—because of their disabilities—won't be able to and can end up feeling as if they are on the outside of the community looking in. Yet showing your support for involvement in these activities is helpful. It's important that your service member learn about the community to which he or she is returning and its present "culture." This kind of "lived" education typically occurs organically; the longer your service member spends in a culture or community, the closer he or she will be to the possibility of transformation. The key is for your service member to be open to this cultural shift and to not withdraw from the community he or she is now a part of.

How You Can Help

If your service member is in the National Guard or Reserves or is a veteran, think broadly of anyone you know who could help him or her reintegrate into the community. Maybe you have developed contacts through work, friendships, school, church, or your neighborhood. There is nothing better than being able to refer your service member to a friend who may be able to connect him or her with a job lead or social group. Your personal relationships may end up being an incredibly valuable asset in your service member's reintegration into civilian life. Rather than only providing your service member with names and phone numbers, consider hosting an event to introduce him or her to some of these people; this can facilitate networking. Sometimes a function like watching a sporting event on TV can be a great way for your service member to connect with an important community contact.

You may also find that your contacts have their own networks that can provide your service member with additional support. In this way, you may be able to expand your network of support for your service member more widely than you thought. Remember, however, that such new contacts, being less personally connected with your service member, are typically less driven to help, so you might have to work harder to obtain their follow-through.

Conclusion

It's important to think of reintegration as a multipronged process in which your service member, family, and community reach out toward each other in ways that will benefit all of you. While we can't return our troops to their former selves after deployment, we can help them use this life-changing experience to find new possibilities for growth and connection.

Chapter Tips

- Everybody changes after being deployed. Expect changes in your service member, and be open and nonjudgmental toward them.
- Your service member may *never* want to talk with you about his or her deployment. That's okay. Don't push and pry.
- Your service member may want to deploy again as soon as possible. If so, don't take it personally. For some, life is simply more meaningful on deployment.
- Readjusting can take much longer than a few weeks, particularly for members of the National Guard or Reserves. Be patient and supportive.
- It can take time for your service member to emotionally reconnect with you. Don't rush it. Appreciate all your son or daughter has been through and reevaluate your expectations.
- Facilitate communication by inviting your service member to share photos, videos, and other memorabilia from his or her deployment.
- Help your service member see how unhealthy habits are negatively affecting his or her life and learn to use positive military values as a catalyst for change.

- Take advantage of your personal contacts to help your service member reintegrate, and encourage involvement in community events.
- For some suggested sources of further information and support, turn to the list of resources at the back of the book.

chapter 2

Professional, Vocational, and Financial Concerns

It's been a tough transition. He's trying to find work and having trouble adjusting to life here again. (Olivia)

Transitioning from overseas deployment to stateside life poses a number of challenges for most service members, whether they are returning to a base or a civilian community. Transition scenarios vary from simply completing a military contract, or being boarded out due to a medical disability, to retiring after twenty or more years of military service. Those who find themselves back on base in a "desk job" also face challenging transitions; so do those in the National Guard or Reserves who return to a previously held position of civilian employment, as well as those who face unemployment and those who decide to continue their education.

Although the issues facing service members are different in each of these scenarios, in this chapter we'll outline some of the common practical challenges related to employment, school, and finances. We'll then provide suggestions for tackling these issues, including whether and how you should get involved and strategies for talking to your service member about these practical concerns.

Obtaining or Returning to Employment

He just got back and is so confused about what he wants to do—he doesn't know whether he should get a job or go to school. (Jose)

Service members who leave active duty after returning home often find it difficult to obtain or return to employment. As of this writing, male veterans between the ages of eighteen and twenty-four have a 29.1 percent unemployment rate, compared to 17.6 percent among a group of young male nonveterans (BLS 2012). This difference may in part be due to misinformation or misperceptions employers have about returning service members. For example, an employer may question a recently deployed service member's mental stability: "Is he one of those crazy veterans? Will he go ballistic? Can I talk with him?" Veterans may also not know how best to present themselves and their military service to prospective employers.

Members of the National Guard or Reserves may be concerned that an employer will be less interested in hiring them if they disclose their current military status and their need to occasionally miss work because of training obligations or even a deployment. While military values like commitment to the mission and one's duty, honor and integrity, courage, discipline, and loyalty are extremely useful from an employer standpoint, service members can struggle to communicate these values both on their résumé and in interviews. Additionally, it may be a challenge to adequately transfer the skills and knowledge gained from military service more generally, and a military occupation specifically, to civilian employment. How does the skill set of an infantryman, sniper, or explosives specialist translate to the civilian job market?

Getting Help with Employment

I'm more the support system and encourager unless she asks me for advice. (Victoria)

While some parents have expertise in the area of finding employment and can directly help their service member, most don't. Even if you have the know-how, your service member may not be able to take your advice or discuss career aspirations with you, for various reasons. If this is the case, he or she may benefit from working with a career or employment counselor. As well as help with job placement, a good career or employment counselor can help your veteran examine his or her interests and aptitudes, write résumés and cover letters, and practice interview techniques.

You can locate a career or employment counselor through the federal government (both the Veterans Health Administration and the Veterans Benefits Administration have some career services) or through local nonprofit or for-profit organizations that specialize in job placement. For example, Swords to Plowshares, a San Francisco Bay Area–based veterans' organization, provides employment services to veterans and offers training and certification (sometimes in coordination with schools) for veterans in areas such as clean energy, transportation, health care, and security. It's critical that the counselor helping your service member be someone who knows veterans' issues, is knowledgeable about many careers, has referral connections for job interviews, and is easy to work with. Remember that veterans, and disabled veterans in particular, have an edge when applying for federal employment.

Additionally, there are a number of websites geared toward assisting service members in search of employment. For example, the Department of Labor's Transition Assistance Program (TAP) (www.dol.gov/vets/programs/tap) provides employment and training information to service members and their spouses within one year of separation from the military or two years of retirement. TAP also conducts three-day workshops on military bases covering a wide variety of topics related to obtaining employment (DOL 2012). VA for Vets provides a variety of services for veterans who are interested in a career within the federal government, and the website (vaforvets.va.gov) offers tips for reintegration as well as résumé-building documents.

When it comes time to apply for a job, a résumé that highlights your service member's unique military experience, strongly held military values, ability to handle a high level of responsibility (e.g., being in charge of multimillion-dollar equipment, leading a platoon on convoys several times a week for months), and exposure to all kinds of stressors and demands can help land an interview. Therefore, your service member may want to take advantage of those websites that promote résumé-writing for veterans or turn to vocational counselors available through the Department of Veterans Affairs (VA) who can also help with this task. In addition to the federal government, some private organizations and companies like Hire Heroes USA (http.hireheroesusa.org) and CareerPro Global (www.militaryresumewriters.com) sponsor résumé-writing workshops for veterans. Another option amenable to some service members is to sit down with a family member, a family friend, a former teacher, or a mentor to write a résumé together. Above all, your service member should be encouraged to spend adequate time in preparation and to have someone with a good editorial eye review his or her résumé before applying for a job.

Certain companies like Walmart and Tesla Motors are very active in recruiting and hiring veterans, so your service member may want to target veteran-friendly organizations such as these in his or her job search. In addition, Google has a comprehensive website entitled "Google for Veterans and Families" (www.googleforveterans.com). This site has an entire section devoted to exploring life after military service (under "Tools for Veterans"), allowing those who sign up to build a résumé, develop a financial plan, and develop an online business presence.

> *[I would recommend parents] become aware of veterans outreach, the veterans college counselors, organizations who will train and hire vets.... Give them the support and confidence they look for when facing a great adjustment in their lives.* (Dan)

Workplace Challenges

Your service member found a job! Terrific! You can all relax now, right? Not necessarily—in fact, reintegration is just beginning. Even after your service member has found employment, he or she may face unforeseen challenges. Service members who find employment in entry-level positions may have a difficult time determining how to respond to common employer demands. Military service and particularly deployment can alter how your son or daughter understands and responds to requests made by a civilian employer. Some service members respond to assigned tasks with an overdose of seriousness and rigidity, while others may not take their employer's concerns seriously enough. For example, your daughter may work hard but not connect well with her coworkers, giving the appearance of not being a "team player" and thereby hurting her chances for advancement. Or your son may have a boss who treats deadlines as life-or-death situations, while deployment has given your son a vastly different sense of what's important. Or a military level of dedication to the mission may not exist within a business organization, leaving your service member unsure of how much effort to put forth in support of the business.

As we mentioned earlier, service members may also struggle to find that "high" or sense of purpose they used to get from their military job, which may partially explain why many former service members end up in emergency responder positions (e.g., police, fire, EMT, disaster planning) and why some members of the National Guard or Reserves consider moving to full-time military status.

Going to School

Ellen served two tours in Afghanistan prior to returning home to live with her mother. She enrolled in community college, taking a heavy course load. Ellen quickly realized that she was not able to focus and retain information as well as she had in the past. She had taken on too much but preferred to "suck it up" and not let anyone know, leading her to fail a couple of classes. She finally let her mom and professors know that she was having difficulty concentrating at school. She was then referred to the school's disabled student services, where they identified her problem and worked with her to develop appropriate accommodations, improving her school performance and lowering her stress level.

While some entered the military with the goal of earning their college tuition and housing through the GI Bill, others return from deployment not knowing what to do next. Many returning service members are not mentally or experientially ready to go straight into the job market. Enrolling in some kind of schooling can provide them with intellectual stimulation, focus, goals, a sense of purpose, and exposure to a number of job or career possibilities that can help determine their direction. If your service member is considering further education, he or she will need to choose between an online and a "brick and mortar" school, or some combination of the two, as well as the level and/or type of school (e.g., vocational school, community college, university) to attend.

Choosing a Program

Online programs are often very convenient and therefore have become increasingly popular. However, they typically don't provide as much community support as brick-and-mortar schools, which interestingly are themselves developing more online curricula. The online option can be especially useful for those who live in rural areas, are already employed, or are unable to get into the courses they want at their community college or university. For service members who are struggling to adapt to busy, crowded environments or who feel anxious about the idea of sitting for hours in a classroom, online courses can seem less threatening. Ideally, however, such students should gradually transition to attending classes on campus, as this will help them develop coping skills and increase their social engagement. According to the report *Military Service Members and Veterans in Higher Education; What the New GI Bill May Mean for Postsecondary Institutions* (Radford 2009), in 2008, approximately 4 percent of US undergraduate students were veterans, with a growing number of female veterans.

For some, military service and deployment in particular provides an opportunity to discover aptitudes and develop skills in fields that they had not previously considered. Your service member may return with a sudden passion for machine mechanics or even cooking and may choose to attend a vocational or professional school as a pathway into that particular job market. If you had hoped that your service member would obtain a university degree, you may feel disappointed by this decision. It's important, however, to remember that deployment can have a significant impact on identity development and that your service member's struggle to adjust after deployment may be pulling him or her to do what "feels right." Who knows—you might wind up with a world-class chef in the family! It may also be that as your service member continues to reintegrate into civilian life, his or her priorities and passions will shift again, in a direction that you are more comfortable with.

Many service members, having learned a number of skills including self-discipline and perseverance, do incredibly well in school. However, like employment, the transition to school can pose challenges. The school environment is significantly different from military life. Initially, your service member may not fit in or may feel very different from other students. School in general is a much less structured environment than the military, and that means there is a great deal of built-in "free" time. Unstructured time can be a welcome relief but also a double-edged sword for some service members. They may rebel against using the self-discipline they were taught in the military and fall behind in schoolwork. Even students who did well previously, like Ellen described earlier, may have a psychological or medical problem related to their military service that makes studying and paying attention in class difficult.

If your service member wasn't a good student prior to entering the military, he or she may have an undiagnosed learning disability. Anxiety about school performance can compound these difficulties. In addition, if your service member hasn't been in school for a while, he or she may be out of sync with professors' expectations or requirements or more used to real-world, hands-on military training than classroom learning and test taking. On the other hand, we've also seen students who didn't take school seriously before entering the military later excel at it.

Different from Peers

My son seems very much unchanged in his manner and style, but he has lost patience with others his own age that are not doing anything with their lives and complain or act entitled without doing anything. (Holden)

Because students who are veterans don't wear military uniforms, they generally don't stand out in a crowd. However, your service member will most likely be older, have more life experience, and be more serious about school than his or her classmates. Difficulty relating to fellow students can make working with them on group assignments especially challenging.

In class, professors sometimes ask students to talk about themselves, which can pose a dilemma for service members. For instance, being open about military experience or a recent deployment may mean having to endure a number of awkward and/or inappropriate questions or political comments about war, like "Did you kill anybody?" Even service members who don't share their military experience are still subject to hearing conversations across the political spectrum. These conversations can trigger powerful memories of deployment or may lead to negative feelings, either toward classmates or about having served.

Service members may also become irritated at what some of their typically younger fellow students take for granted. For example, your daughter who has earned the GI Bill may believe that her peers whose parents pay for their schooling do not appreciate the opportunities they have been given. On the flip side, other students who are working and taking out loans in order to attend may be resentful of your service member's earned benefits without an understanding or appreciation of the sacrifice he or she has made.

Different from the Military

Brad, a twenty-four-year-old Army veteran who had served in both Iraq and Afghanistan, found himself at an art institute with eighteen- and nineteen-year-olds who had no clue about the wars going on in the Middle East. He didn't let anyone on campus know he'd served in the military, since he was certain they wouldn't be able to relate to his experience. A few times at school, when Brad was in large crowds or passing through the student union where war-related news was blasting from the big-screen TVs, he felt a surge of anxiety and began scanning for "the enemy." He felt like a foreign student in his own country.

The rules regarding free speech on campus are in sharp contrast to what is tolerated in the military, with varying views on war and on the military being not only accepted, but also encouraged. Class discussions on political or social issues can be unsettling or even trigger traumatic memories for service members. In the college environment, thinking "outside the box" and challenging conventional wisdom and conventional speech ideals may be welcomed and rewarded, which in many cases is in direct conflict with military culture. This can add to feelings of alienation that student veterans may experience at home or in the community.

At a practical level, newly returned service members can be overwhelmed by having to navigate the decentralized system of campus life as compared to the military—in which they were told what to do, where to go, and even what to wear and what to eat.

Some Schools Are Aware

Samantha was attending community college after recently being discharged from the Air Force. Luckily she found her way to the veterans club on campus, where, surrounded by former service members, she immediately felt at home. "Having this club on campus really helps me feel safe," she said. "I know these guys have my back."

Fortunately, more and more schools are providing services to help veterans successfully transition from military life to the classroom. Many schools provide priority registration if veterans request it and bring in a copy of their DD214 (military record) as proof of their service, regardless of whether they are eligible for additional benefits.

A number of schools are also developing resource centers for veterans or places for veterans to congregate on campus, such as student veterans clubs. Here veterans may socialize, support one another, study, and share their experiences and insights regarding veteran-friendly professors and courses, as well as information about how the school's veteran services work.

Excellent entry-level classes for veterans that specifically address the challenges of reintegration are available on some college and university campuses. These classes cover everything from study skills and writing strategies to negotiating the GI Bill and even mental health issues. Also, sometimes English and philosophy departments, for example, offer classes that focus on veterans' issues. These classes, the composition of which varies from veteran-only to a mix of veterans and nonveterans, can provide an opportunity for veterans to share their experiences through writing, oral presentations, or dialogue with other students. They can also provide veterans a welcome respite from the stress of unfamiliar surroundings and pressure to "fit in."

There are also approved "Yellow Ribbon" schools that, along with the VA, help pay tuition that exceeds established limits under the Post-9/11 GI Bill. For more information and to determine eligibility, visit the GI Bill Web Site at gibill.va.gov/gi_bill_info/ch33/yrp/yrp_list_2010.htm.

Student Veteran Services Make a Difference

I do not know if most people understand the sacrifice our young military men and women endure. They don't understand the minimal wages a young recruit makes or why they should get college funds under the GI Bill. They don't understand the miserable conditions they live under, and the long hours with no time off. (Seiko)

Some schools provide excellent campus-based veteran services, including a Certifying Official (veteran advocate), as well as veteran academic counselors who help service members think through course requirements, making sure that the classes they select fit within their GI Bill benefits. For more information on GI Bill benefits, visit the VA's website at gibill.va.gov. National organizations like the Student Veterans of America (SVA) (www.studentveterans.org) provide camaraderie, support, and advocacy for student veterans.

Service members can earn college credit for military training and experience depending on their military occupational specialty, so it's important that they know of this possibility and check it out when meeting with a veteran advocate like a Certifying Official before enrolling in classes. The American Council on Education (ACE) helps coordinate between the Department of Defense (DoD) and higher education to determine what military training counts as course credit. For more information, visit the American Council on Education at http.acenet.edu/higher-education/Pages/Military-Students-and-Veterans.aspx.

Furthermore, the Veterans Health Administration's (VHA's) Mental Health Services has attempted to address issues and difficulties facing student veterans through an innovative program called Veteran Integration To Academic Leadership (VITAL). VITAL, now on over twenty campuses across the country, provides an array of outreach services to student veterans including enrollment in VHA health care, education about benefits and college services, mental health counseling, and social services. VITAL also educates faculty and staff on military culture and helps address issues that arise for student veterans on campus. The variety of services provided decreases the barriers for student veterans and may help improve their school performance. Some of the VHAs that work closely with schools are Ann Arbor, Michigan; Austin, Texas; Bedford, Massachusetts; San Francisco, California; and Tuscaloosa, Alabama.

There are also "VetSuccess" programs supported by the Veterans Benefits Administration that provide services—primarily vocational rehabilitation counseling—to eligible veterans on college campuses. For more information, go to vetsuccess.gov/vetsuccess.

Services for Disabled Students

Most schools (by law) have services for students with any of a number of physical or mental health–related disabilities, including learning problems associated with diagnosed medical or mental health conditions (e.g., lower back pain, tinnitus, attention deficit disorder, traumatic brain injury, depression, anxiety, post-traumatic stress). While these services can be very beneficial for student veterans like Ellen, it requires some work and self-advocacy to secure them and to ensure that the accommodations are being provided. In order to be eligible, students typically need to have a mental health or medical professional provide a diagnosis and recommend appropriate accommodations and/or services (generally via a form provided by the school). In some instances, service members may be asked to undergo an evaluation at the school or at their local VHA, if enrolled, and then authorize the release of that information to their school.

Although the services available to veterans with disabilities will vary depending on the school, here are some examples:

- A note-taker
- Audio equipment to record lectures
- An environment with reduced distractions in which to take tests, quizzes, and final exams
- Extended time to take tests
- Preferential seating (either at the front of the classroom, if the primary issue is distraction or hearing, or at the back of the classroom, for veterans who feel uncomfortable with others sitting behind them or not being able to see the entrance/exits)

- "Smart pens," which look like pens but can record what you are writing on a special notebook, linking your written notes to the appropriate section of the lecture

Your service member may be unaware of such options or may be reluctant to take advantage of them. Unfortunately, some student veterans recognize that help is needed only after seeing hard evidence of their academic struggles: the negative impact on their grade point average. Consequently a good strategy for parents is to provide proactive support as tactfully as possible. One way to do this is to begin by encouraging your service member to seek out less stigmatizing accommodations, such as for physical problems. Some schools may provide a special padded chair for students with documented problems such as lower back pain, which is very common among service members due to the weight of military gear. Once your service member knows where to go for help, he or she may be more likely to raise more sensitive concerns (e.g., being easily distracted or hypervigilant due to post-traumatic stress).

An additional issue is letting professors know about the accommodations once they are approved. Students requesting accommodations do not need to disclose their specific disability to their instructors, but must show their instructors evidence of approved accommodations. Be aware that there is usually a deadline for arranging testing accommodations (e.g., a week before a test, a month before the final exam).

Questions and Answers about School

Should I encourage my son to talk to his professors about his military service if he is having trouble in school?

There are certain circumstances in which your son will need to discuss his military service; for example, when a drill interferes with a weekend assignment. Excluding these kinds of situations, there isn't a clear answer to this question. While some professors are incredibly supportive of student veterans, some may be unsupportive and even quietly (or not so quietly) prejudicial. There are numerous examples of professors going the extra mile for veterans by mentoring and assisting them with course material, as well as helping them obtain additional academic or even mental health services. However, there are also professors who have been less than helpful and even hostile toward veterans. If your son believes that a professor has treated him unfairly, he should speak with the Dean of Students (or go through the appropriate chain of command at the school). Your son also has the option of evaluating his professor through websites like Rate My Professors (www.ratemyprofessors.com) to communicate any concerns to veterans considering taking that class in the future. Other veterans further along in their education may also be a great resource or mentor, as they can help steer your son to the most appropriate professors.

If my daughter has school problems, how will they affect her benefits?

Because of the current requirements of the GI Bill, if your daughter is struggling academically, it may be financially advantageous for your daughter to fail a class rather than withdraw. If your daughter needs to withdraw from a class, she will be obligated to pay back the government, which is not the case if she fails (as long as she continues to attend the class through the end of the semester or quarter). If your daughter stops attending a class (even if she does not officially withdraw), she will still need to pay for the portion of the course remaining. Prior to making any decision, strongly encourage your daughter to speak with the Certifying Official or an academic counselor familiar with veteran benefits about available options. Additionally, veterans who choose to fail a class rather than withdraw should communicate this intention to their professor. Most instructors are usually willing to accommodate a veteran's desire not to withdraw from the class, but the instructor may need to provide documentation to the Certifying Official that the student was in attendance through the end of the semester or quarter. As a general rule, encouraging your daughter to stay in communication with instructors, the Certifying Official, and the academic adviser can help prevent or mitigate problems.

How can I help my service member be successful in school?

Probably one of the most important things you can do is encourage your service member to take advantage of any help that he or she qualifies for, whether by virtue of being a veteran or not. Remember, any assistance your service member obtains, whether from the GI Bill or, for example, disabled student services, is help that he or she has earned. How much help you can be as a parent will depend upon your service member's willingness to honestly communicate with you about school. Without honest communication regarding struggles, it's very difficult to develop solutions. If you can get an accurate assessment, then your role typically won't be to solve problems, but to help your service member solve them himself or herself, possibly with some guidance and suggestions from you.

Keep in mind that students are often inundated with information at the beginning of the semester or quarter, so encourage your service member to call or visit the school before starting. Also encourage him or her to identify and meet with the Certifying Official as soon as possible, because that person can provide invaluable guidance regarding the processes and procedures for veterans.

Financial Challenges: The Buck Stops Here

I honor his sacrifice but temper it with tough love when needed. Money has dried up and he has had to make some tough financial choices. (Heather)

In addition to vocational challenges, some service members return from deployment with financial problems. This may be especially true for those in the National Guard or Reserves who took a cut in pay while serving, only to return with significant debt. In some instances, service members' spouses do not manage money effectively in their absence, creating financial instability or even incurring significant debt, which for a parent can be extremely painful to discover.

Other service members, particularly those who are young and single, return with money that they accumulated from combat pay. In the excitement of being home, they may end up treating themselves and/or family members to "fun" items like motorcycles or expensive automobiles or activities like gambling or luxury vacations. While it's a good idea for service members to reward themselves after deployment, if they spend all that they've earned and then some, the resulting financial hole can be hard to climb out of.

In addition, those who separate from service will no longer receive a military housing allowance, comprehensive military health care benefits for themselves and their families, or the opportunity for tax-free deployment and/or hazard pay and other financial perks. Some service members do not qualify for the GI Bill, and even with the GI Bill (which includes a housing allowance), some student veterans find that they still need to take out loans in order to finish school. Additionally, the elimination of break pay (pay received when on break from school) or a housing allowance might result in financial challenges for full-time students during summer and winter breaks, if they have no employment during these times.

These challenges can leave you with a difficult predicament: If your service member has financial problems, should you try to help (assuming that you can)? If you do help, will this enable your service member to continue to spend money in less than responsible ways? How much you help and in what ways will depend on numerous factors, including your own relationship with money. For example, you may determine that because your daughter has not typically asked for financial help in the past, her request is really a cry for help with something else, such as emotional problems. Or you may decide that your son is asking for something he could easily live without. Here are some suggestions to help you deal with these dilemmas:

- Ask your service member to explore alternative ways of solving his or her financial problems—such as obtaining service-connected disability or getting a part-time job.

- Have your service member make a financial request of you in writing. Clearly indicating what is being requested can go a long way toward clarifying the specifics of your financial support.
- If you are offering a loan, draw up a contract that specifies a repayment plan, to help avoid future conflict and frustration.

In general, it can be very useful for your service member to develop some kind of financial plan. Because the military takes care of so many aspects of members' lives, including their housing and family benefits, your service member may have never developed good spending habits or may simply not be accustomed to managing money.

A basic financial plan typically starts with a comparison of income (including items such as savings, pensions, and other assets) and all current expenses (food, housing, utilities, mortgage, child support, car payments, etc.). The process of putting income and expenses down on paper can help your service member consider his or her financial future in concrete terms. By combining this with a discussion of his or her financial goals and dreams, you can help your service member move toward developing a realistic budget.

Maybe you or someone you know has expertise in financial planning. Or maybe an outside expert can help put together a plan that can lead to a more stable financial future for your service member. If you arrange or even pay for a preliminary meeting with a financial consultant, it may pay off in the long run.

Conclusion

Vocational, educational, and financial concerns can impede service members' ability to transition smoothly to life after deployment. Their struggles with everyday practicalities in areas like work and school can lead to a negative sense of themselves and their future. They may ask themselves questions that begin to cast doubt on their view of the world and their abilities, such as *Was deployment worth it?*

and *How is it that I was successful in the military but now can't even find a job?* As a result of such struggles, your service member may come to believe that the "war at home" is more difficult than the battle overseas, putting him or her at risk of developing mental health problems. By helping your service member address these important transitional hurdles, you can minimize that risk.

Chapter Tips

- Work with your service member to determine the type of help he or she needs to be successful in school or to find and keep a job.
- Remind your service member that he or she possesses important skills that can be successfully transferred from the military to school or civilian job settings.
- Make sure that your son or daughter takes advantage of available help. Colleges and universities have many good resources for veterans—the trick is finding them.
- "Bridge the gap" whenever possible by educating others about your service member's experiences. Nonmilitary community members such as employers and professors may not know how to interact with your service member.
- Help your service member develop good financial habits by creating a financial plan.
- Become resource smart. Connect your service member to resources and websites aimed at employment and education for veterans.
- For some suggested sources of further information and support, turn to the list of resources at the back of the book.

chapter 3

Deployment's Toll on the Mind and Spirit: Psychological Injuries and Spiritual Struggles

I feel it [deployment] has changed my son forever. (David)

One of the primary complaints we hear from service members after deployment is that after their first few months back home, friends, family members, and coworkers begin treating them as though they never deployed—acting as though everything is "back to normal," while they themselves are still trying to define what "normal" is after their experience. Fortunately, the majority of military personnel are highly adaptive and resilient individuals who after deployment gradually adjust to what is now being referred to as "The New Normal" (MCEC 2012): a state in which service members have incorporated their deployment experiences to form a new way of looking at themselves and the world. However, for some service members, bad habits formed during or after deployment, such as those discussed in chapter 1, can become entrenched and are potentially symptoms of psychological injuries. In this chapter we move beyond normal readjustment issues and bad habits to common mental health problems experienced by returning service members. We hope that our discussion assists you in detecting any signs and symptoms of psychological injury so that you can support your service member in getting the help that he or she needs. Unfortunately and sometimes quite tragically, service members who experience significant mental health problems often don't seek help until their symptoms seriously interfere with their ability to function in relationships, in their jobs, and in the community.

As the parent of a service member who was deployed, you too may struggle to adjust as you observe changes in your son or daughter that you don't entirely understand. This understanding is key to helping your service member through the healing process, to a place where he or she is able to participate fully in life and relationships. The goal of this chapter is to help you gain a better understanding of your service member's problems and struggles and then offer you concrete strategies to assist in his or her recovery.

If you have concerns that your service member may be having thoughts of suicide go straight to the section titled "Thoughts of Suicide" at the end of this chapter for information on what to look for and how to intervene.

When Bad Habits Become Entrenched

As we discussed in chapter 1, while many bad habits are simply annoying and others are just plain unhealthy, some can be downright destructive. Although for the majority of service members, the initial year of reintegration poses the most challenges, it's generally the second year in which the real cost of wartime deployment begins to show. Problems that at first seemed relatively minor, such as excessive computer use or staying up until dawn, may have come to interfere with relationships and other responsibilities. What initially appeared to be a vice, such as gambling, binge drinking, or medication abuse, may now be a full-blown addiction. Job loss, domestic violence, divorce, and arrests are all potential costs of continued problematic behaviors such as these.

Sleep Problems

Sleep problems are by far the most common complaint of service members after deployment. While they are deployed, service members' sleep is often severely disrupted by working unusual and extended shifts, bunking down in uncomfortable settings, and remaining vigilant to every sound that might signal danger. After returning home, service members can find it difficult to sleep in spite of the fact that they are now in comfortable, secure surroundings. If nothing else, simply the time zone change can cause sleep difficulties. Add to this the pain of physical injuries and the hyperalertness and disturbed awakenings of post-traumatic stress, and your service member's ability to sleep may suffer for a number of reasons.

Unfortunately, sleep disruptions in the initial phase of reintegration can easily turn into chronic problems for service members who unknowingly use ineffective and unhealthy means to get some much-needed rest. Bad habits such as daytime napping, erratic sleep schedules, or excessive caffeine or alcohol can interfere with the body's ability to gradually adjust to stateside sleeping and further fuel insomnia. It's never too late for your service member to get his or her sleep back on track, and there are good treatments out there for sleep problems, including insomnia and nightmares. While it may take discipline and perseverance to break these bad habits, your service member may soon see the benefits of such efforts. In chapter 7 you will find simple tips that can help not only your service member, but also you and your entire family, get a better night's sleep.

If your service member has suffered a psychological injury, disrupted sleep and daytime fatigue are most likely aggravating it. Conversely, a psychological condition may be fueling a sleep problem—for example, your daughter delays sleep for fear of having another nightmare, or your son plays computer games throughout the night to avoid disturbing feelings or memories that arise in the absence of distractions. If your service member is suffering from repeated nightmares (see "Post-Traumatic Stress" later in this chapter), you might suggest a visit to a health care provider to inquire about medications such as prazosin to help reduce the nightmares themselves or lessen the anxiety (and accompanying physical symptoms such as sweating and thrashing) that commonly interferes with sleep. Additionally, imagery rehearsal therapy (IRT), a brief treatment that targets nightmares directly by having individuals rewrite their frightening or distressing dreams and then rehearse these new narratives, has thus far shown promising results for some service members.

Anger

> Ever since Ron got back from his last deployment, he's on a short fuse and explodes without any apparent reason. The littlest things make him really angry. The family and I feel like we're walking on eggshells whenever he's around. Even when we just ask a question like "How was your day?" he gets irritated. The last thing I want to do is make him upset because it scares me. He's gotten violent a few times. So I try not to bother him and instead wind up avoiding him.

In addition to sleep disturbance, another very common post-deployment issue is anger. When military personnel are on deployment, anger often develops as the emotional armor that protects them from feeling helpless and afraid. Anger helps drive human beings to fight, and for that reason it's readily accepted, if not harnessed, in war zones. In the military, where most emotional expression is stigmatized as a sign of weakness, anger exudes power and strength and is therefore tolerated (so long as it's not directed at a superior). Because of this, it's not unusual for service members to express other emotions—guilt, anxiety, even grief—in the form of anger.

As a parent, you may not like to think of your son or daughter as having an anger problem. In fact, you may have considered skipping this section altogether because your service member has never thrown a vase, kicked the dog, or punched a neighbor. But that kind of outright aggression and hostility is only one end of the anger continuum. Signs of irritability or expressions of annoyance, displeasure, or frustration like slamming doors, giving sarcastic responses, or yelling—while these behaviors may not rise to the level of physical violence—can also have their roots in anger.

If you remember your service member as being calm and gentle or not easily irritated prior to deployment, you may be wondering what has happened to set him or her so on edge. It may be that during deployment, everyday frustrations such as limited supplies, extreme weather and living conditions, and inadequate equipment built to a constant state of irritability that your daughter couldn't shake, even after returning home. Or maybe the practical frustrations of reintegration such as unemployment, financial struggles, or unwanted base assignments have sparked a flame of bitterness and resentment that continues to burn in your son even after these issues have been resolved. For those suffering from post-traumatic stress, irritability and anger may simply be a manifestation of hyperarousal, while those who have experienced significant loss may express their grief or even guilt through verbal outbursts.

Regardless of the cause, if your service member's anger problem has continued past the initial year of reintegration, the odds are that it has taken its toll on his or her relationships and career. *Your* relationship may have been particularly affected, since children are often most comfortable unleashing their anger on parents. While this may be true, you should *not* tolerate hurtful outbursts and you should *never* accept physical violence, regardless of your service member's psychological injuries. Anger has a way of building and can spiral out of control if left unchecked.

This does not mean, however, that it's up to you to manage your service member's anger problem. There are numerous anger management programs available through Veterans Health Administration (VHA) Medical Centers, Community-Based Outpatient Clinics, and Vet Centers as well as self-help books such as our first book, *Courage After Fire*. Again, your service member does not need to be at the point of physical violence to make use of these resources. In fact, it's best to address anger *before* it reaches the point of aggressive behavior.

While it's up to your service member to manage his or her own anger, you can take responsibility for how you respond. Here are some tips:

- **Set limits.** Be clear with your service member about what you will and will not tolerate. Don't make vague comments such as "I don't like it when you're angry." Instead, be as concrete as possible by identifying specific behaviors and how you intend to respond to them in the future. For example, "If you chase after a driver who has cut you off, I will no longer ride with you as a passenger"; "If you scream at me, I will end the conversation and leave the room until you've calmed down"; "If you grab my arm or push me, you can no longer live in this house." Discuss these limits only when your service member is calm—this means not until at least thirty minutes after an angry outburst. You may find that by waiting until you are both calm, you can launch a productive conversation about the impact of your service member's anger on you and other loved ones. As you no doubt learned in your early years of parenting, the most important and difficult part of setting limits is the follow-through. Be prepared to back up your words with action, or you run the risk of reinforcing the very behaviors that you are trying to prevent.

- **Manage your reactions.** It's inevitable that you will experience an emotional response to your service member's anger. This is especially true in families with a history of conflict and reactivity prior to deployment. If you yourself are prone to anger, you may want to seek out your own anger management resources. Even if it's a verbal argument, meeting anger with anger can only lead to an escalation that one or both of you will regret. When your service member's anger turns physical, an aggressive reaction on your part can be just plain dangerous.

  If you tend to feel fearful or highly anxious in the presence of another's anger, utilize strategies like slow breathing to manage your anxiety both during the confrontation and afterward. You will find an example of a slow breathing exercise in chapter 7. (Remember that if you practice this strategy during times when you are not particularly anxious, you will find that it comes to you more easily and works more effectively in times of crisis.) It may be that you have had extreme anger or violence directed at you in the past. If so, your service member's expressions of anger may bring up distressing memories and feelings. If this is the case, you may benefit from seeing a counselor or therapist who can help you process these memories and manage the emotions that they bring.

- **Be vigilant about violence.** Even if your service member has not been physically violent toward you, there may be signs that his or her anger is spiraling out of control. Perhaps your service member returns home at night with telltale cuts and bruises from a fistfight. Maybe your service member's partner (e.g., spouse) or child has unexplained injuries or is oddly absent from family functions. As you may know, rates of family violence increase significantly following war-zone deployment (Hoge, Castro, and Eaton 2004), and if your service member suffers from post-traumatic stress, the risk is even greater. This means that even if your service member has never been violent before, there's a possibility that he or she is now expressing anger through physical aggression. It's therefore important that you maintain close contact with your service member's partner and not allow suspicious injuries or absences to go unchecked. Trust your instincts. If you are ever concerned for anyone's safety, do not hesitate to call 911. As difficult as this may be, preventing family violence will only benefit your service member, as well as his or her loved ones.

Staying Safe

Being vigilant about violence means being aware of when your personal safety is threatened. If your service member has been aggressive toward you in any way, such as throwing objects in your direction, shoving you out of the way, roughly grabbing your arm, or making verbal threats, have a plan for what to do and where to go if you're ever feeling unsafe. The first step in your plan should be to get away, even if it means getting out of a car or leaving your own home. Be sure you have a clear idea of whom to call or alternatively where to go if you don't have immediate access to a phone. Maybe there is a particular neighbor whom you trust or a nearby store where you can get help. *Again, do not hesitate to call 911 if you believe that you are in danger and cannot immediately get to a safe place.*

Alcohol Problems

My daughter is having some symptoms of PTSD; is angry, some depression; when things get really stressful for her, it's easy to turn to alcohol. (Ashton)

Many service members commonly use alcohol to relax and have fun. However, those who have been exposed to upsetting or traumatic events may be at risk for alcohol problems. Additional reasons for service members to use alcohol after deployment include:

- To avoid thinking about upsetting things that happened during deployment
- To avoid disturbing feelings like depression, guilt, shame, or grief
- To feel less tense and jumpy
- To feel more comfortable in crowds or social situations
- To get to sleep and fend off nightmares

But as you probably are aware, not all drinking is problem drinking. So how do you know when your service member's alcohol use has turned to abuse? Here are some signs of problem drinking:

- Failing to fulfill responsibilities (e.g., calling in sick because of a hangover, going out drinking instead of studying)
- Blackouts or memory loss during periods of drinking

- Sneaking or lying about alcohol use
- Increased aggression or depression while drinking (e.g., getting into fights, expressing thoughts of death)
- Driving while intoxicated
- Drinking in the morning
- Spending limited resources on alcohol rather than practical needs

So what should you do once you've identified that your service member has a drinking problem? As much as you might want to control his or her drinking, just as we said above for anger problems, it's not your job to manage your service member's alcohol use. But also just as with anger, it's most certainly your job to let your service member know how his or her alcohol use has affected your relationship.

You might start by saying something like **"I'm concerned about your drinking. Over the past ____ months/years I've seen alcohol become a problem in your life. (Give concrete examples of times when alcohol has interfered with work, school, or relationships). I understand that you've been using alcohol to feel better since you returned from your deployment, but I'm wondering whether we could start to talk about your alcohol use and how it's affecting you. I'm happy to help you find programs and resources to assist you in decreasing your drinking."**

If your service member is currently active duty, you may want to discuss with him or her the potential repercussions of continued alcohol use. This may include a conversation about how drinking may cause him or her to let his or her buddies down if it leads to demotion or discharge. The Army, Air Force, and Navy (which provides medical and mental health care to both Navy personnel and Marines) all have substance abuse programs: currently, these are the Army Substance Abuse Program (ASAP), the Air Force Alcohol and Drug Abuse Prevention and Treatment (ADAPT) Program, and the Navy Substance Abuse Rehabilitation Program (SARP). VHA hospitals offer substance abuse services as well.

If your service member is not willing to stop or cut down on drinking, you may want to consider setting limits around his or her alcohol use. This is particularly important if your service member has become aggressive or has engaged in dangerous behavior while intoxicated. If your service member lives in your home or visits on a regular basis, the following are examples of limits you might set depending upon the severity of your service member's alcohol problem.

- "You must leave your car at home when you go out."
- "You can't have more than two drinks when we are out to dinner or at a family gathering."
- "You can't keep alcohol in my/our house."
- "Drunken behavior will lose you the privilege of living here."
- "If you don't stop drinking and get treatment, we will no longer assist you financially."

It can be helpful to discuss and agree upon these limits with your partner or your service member's other parent—even if you're no longer a couple—to be sure that you're working together to support your son or daughter. If your service member is married or in a committed relationship, consider sharing your concerns as well as these limits with his or her partner.

Drug Use

Illegal drug use is not tolerated within the military regardless of a service member's location, and random urine screens are conducted to check for such use. However, service members may have had access not only to alcohol but to illicit drugs, prescription drugs, and substances that mimic drugs, like "spice" (synthetic cannabis) during deployment. They may also have even greater access to these after they return home. If your service member is using drugs (including prescription drugs, if used other than as directed), this could be a sign that he or she is struggling with some type of life stressor and/or a deployment-related psychological injury.

Adopting a zero-tolerance policy on illicit drug use (just like the military) will benefit your service member in the long run. Let your service member know that whether he or she is using illicit drugs or abusing prescription drugs to get to sleep, to feel happier, to block out painful memories, or to reduce anxiety, there are better, safer alternatives, many of which we discuss below. Be firm in your expectation that your service member will discontinue the drug use while at the same time offering support and assistance in finding proper help. If your service member is having difficulty managing his or her use of prescribed pain medications, turn to chapter 4 for suggestions on how to help.

Other Problem Behaviors

In chapter 1 we discussed problem behaviors such as pornography, gambling, and excessive Internet use or gaming following deployment. Other seemingly mild but nonetheless detrimental activities are binge or excessive eating, and excessive dieting or purging. If these behaviors have continued beyond the initial year of reintegration, the odds are that they are interfering with your service member's life in the form of financial problems, health problems, or broken relationships. Take these behaviors seriously because like alcohol or drug problems, they are generally indicative of a psychological injury such as those discussed below. Again, you should not hesitate to raise your concerns, providing examples of how your service member's behavior has caused problems in his or her life and relationships. Ideally, this will open the door to a deeper discussion about your service member's readjustment issues and the psychological injuries that resulted from his or her deployment. In chapter 1 you will find a more detailed discussion of how you can help curb or change these unhealthy behaviors.

Injuries of the Mind

> *Don't be afraid to discuss feelings even if they hover too close around issues such as suicide for example. Don't be afraid of what you might hear. The unknown is almost always worse than the known.* (Courtney)

As you know, thinking and talking about feelings like anxiety or sadness or feeling out of control does not come easily to someone who has adopted the military mind-set. You may be part of the military culture yourself and feel a bit uneasy whenever someone mentions "mental health." But when we talk about mental health problems that developed out of experiences during deployment, keep in mind that these are actual *injuries*. Just as your service member may have suffered hearing loss, burns, or a concussion from an IED blast, which we will discuss in chapter 4, he or she may have incurred psychological injuries as well. But unlike physical injuries, psychological injuries are largely invisible and may be particularly difficult to detect in service members, because military personnel often deny or even hide emotional wounds. As a parent, you may be the person most likely to notice subtle changes in your service member's demeanor or behavior. The primary aim of this section is to provide you with strategies for identifying the signs that your service member has suffered a psychological injury and addressing these wounds in the most supportive and effective manner possible.

We understand that you may already be fully aware of your service member's injuries and currently seeking guidance in how to best support him or her. Maybe your daughter was diagnosed and treated during deployment or given a medical discharge because her psychological injuries interfered with her ability to fulfill her duties. Or maybe your son experienced significant problems soon after returning and is now receiving services through military clinics, the Department of Veterans Affairs (VA), or community resources. If your service member's psychological injury has already been identified and you are looking to better understand his or her condition, you may find it most helpful to skip ahead in our discussion to find where we address the specific problem he or she is suffering from.

In the previous section, we reviewed several problem behaviors that may develop after a service member has been deployed. As we mentioned, many if not all of these behaviors may be signs or symptoms of a greater psychological injury. While the trauma and stress of war or other deployment experiences can contribute to a number of mental health conditions, they generally fall within the two main categories of anxiety and depression.

Anxiety

What do people mean when they say they're feeling "anxious"? The general assumption is that they are nervous or apprehensive. Maybe they're starting a new job, taking a test, or going somewhere unfamiliar. Even at this level, anxiety is uncomfortable. We all might recall times of anxiety when we felt butterflies in our stomach or maybe even a slight tremor in our hands. But like anger, anxiety is a continuum, with nervousness at one end and sheer panic at the other.

It's understandable and pretty much expected that service members will experience some level of anxiety during deployment. But for some, repeated exposure to threat and trauma can cause a psychological injury that remains even after they are safe at home. This deployment-related injury most commonly takes one of three forms:

- **Generalized anxiety:** A chronic state of worry
- **Panic attacks:** Episodes of a sudden feeling of fear, accompanied by acute physical symptoms of anxiety
- **Post-traumatic stress:** A reaction to a traumatic experience(s) that includes distressing memories, avoidance of memories and uncomfortable feelings, and physical arousal

It may be that your service member has been seriously affected by one or a combination of these injuries and is already receiving treatment. If not, he or she may be suffering in silence, struggling to manage or even hide such a "weakness," possibly out of fear of jeopardizing his or her military career. Some service members with post-deployment anxiety improve on their own during the first year or two of reintegration and later experience only periodic "flare-ups" during times of stress. While each of these injuries (generalized anxiety, panic attacks, or post-traumatic stress) can range from mild to severe and may even wax and wane over time, it's important that you be aware of their signs and symptoms and familiarize yourself with strategies that will help you support your service member as effectively as possible.

Generalized Anxiety

Friends and family used to describe Trent as "laid back." In fact, his favorite thing to say was "Relax, it's no big deal." But since returning from Afghanistan he has become a "worrier." He spends a lot of time thinking about all the things that could possibly go wrong and is especially concerned about the health and safety of his wife and children.

Worrying is just part of human nature. It's what we do when we're concerned about our finances or about whether we'll make it on time to our next appointment. We worry about the safety of our loved ones when they're in a potentially dangerous situation. But there's a difference between normal worry and *generalized anxiety*.

Normal Worry	Generalized Anxiety
Your worries are focused on a small number of practical concerns.	Your worries involve a wide range of vague concerns.
Your worries don't interfere with your ability to meet responsibilities or complete tasks.	Your worries significantly impair your ability to focus and complete tasks.
You are generally able to set aside your worries to enjoy activities and relationships.	Your worries cause you significant distress and interfere with activities and relationships.
You generally believe that things will turn out okay.	You generally expect the worst to happen.

As you can see, generalized anxiety develops when normal worry, which may have begun with practical concerns, becomes *generalized* to include a wide variety of pitfalls or potential problems. In some cases, this worry simply takes the form of a vague dread without any specific concern to anchor it. For your service member, the consistent yet practical worries of deployment may have now generalized to a chronic expectation that something is going to go wrong. In fact, some things may have indeed gone horribly wrong during deployment, leaving your service member to now expect the worst in everything. While this aura of negativity can be present in depression as well, in generalized anxiety it's accompanied by a state of stress and tension that can at times reach the level of paralyzing fear.

In an effort to fend off these uncomfortable feelings of tension, your service member may be avoiding certain tasks, places, or activities or even avoiding leaving the house. You may also find that your service member's worries have extended to you and other loved ones. Perhaps your daughter repeatedly inquires about your health and prods you to go for a checkup. Or maybe your son worries about you driving and thus thinks of reasons why you shouldn't go out. Your service member may simply call you or drop by several times a day, to "see how you're doing." Other signs that your service member is suffering from generalized anxiety are difficulty getting to sleep or staying asleep because of persistent worry; physical signs of stress such as diarrhea, acid reflux, or muscle tension; and difficulty focusing and concentrating.

If you think that your service member is suffering from generalized anxiety, first remember that no matter how irrational his or her concerns seem, it will not help to say that he or she is being "unreasonable" or "ridiculous." In some cases, those with anxiety know that their worries are irrational, but are still unable to shake the feeling of dread. You probably remember your service member as being a rational person who did not become overwhelmed by small risk potentials. Your goal can be to bring out and build up that rational side until it overpowers the feelings of anxiety and dread. While remaining sympathetic to your service member's worries, try asking some questions that will help kick-start his or her rational thinking:

- "What are the odds that that might happen?"
- "Have you ever had that happen before?"
- "What are the pros and cons (potential benefits and costs) of doing this?"
- "Do you think you might be confusing a feeling with a fact?"
- "Are you thinking in terms of certainties instead of probabilities?"

For instance, if your daughter is anxious about going to the movie theater because "something bad might happen," you might challenge that worry by asking her to consider the odds or the evidence for that belief.

Panic Attacks

While generalized anxiety is a persistent state of worry, panic attacks come on quite suddenly and often unexpectedly. Just as your service member may have had practical worries during deployment turn into an overriding sense of doom at home, his or her fears and sense of threat during deployment may have converted into surges of panic in seemingly safe or ordinary situations. Some military personnel have their first panic attack during deployment or soon after they return, while others don't have this experience until months if not years after deployment. For those who suffer from post-traumatic stress (see below), panic attacks may occur in response to reminders of their traumatic experience(s).

When exposed to an actual threat, the human body naturally responds in preparation for either self-defense or escape. Think of this physical reaction as simple panic: the instinct to fight or run away. A panic attack happens when this physical reaction and the thoughts that accompany it feel overwhelming. In essence, the person is *panicking about panicking*. Panic attacks can be particularly disturbing because they generally occur in objectively nonthreatening environments such as the grocery store, a movie theater, or even home. Here are some examples of physical sensations and how they are interpreted during a panic attack:

Physical Symptom	Cognitive Symptom (Thought)
Accelerated heart rate	*I'm having a heart attack.*
Accelerated respiration (hyperventilation)	*I can't get enough air.*
Dizziness	*I'm going to pass out.*
Uncontrolled shaking	*I'm losing control.*
Nausea	*I'm going to vomit.*

While your service member may have experienced the majority of his or her panic attacks in crowded situations or in reaction to reminders of traumatic experiences, panic attacks are largely unpredictable. Unfortunately this unpredictability often causes panic sufferers to avoid a variety of situations for fear of another attack. For some, this avoidance can be debilitating, compelling them to remain at home and refrain from any activities that might cause them even the smallest amount of anxiety.

Managing a panic attack. If your service member suffers from panic attacks, talk with him or her when panic strikes. Ask what it feels like and whether there's anything that you can do to help. If for example your son says that he would prefer that you not touch him or ask whether he's okay, you can just sit with him quietly until he gets through it.

During a panic attack, a person may benefit from having someone to "breathe with." Ask your service member to focus on and match your breathing as you take slow, steady breaths in and out. Some find breathing into a paper bag helps them slow and control their breathing rate. If this works for your service member, be sure to always have paper bags on hand to help control a panic attack as soon as it arises.

Still others may need to hear words of reassurance that interrupt their steady stream of cognitive symptoms. Phrases like "You're safe," "You can get through this," and "Everything's going to be okay" can be very calming, especially coming from a parent. If your service member's panic attacks prove difficult to manage, intensive cognitive behavioral treatments available at military treatment and VA facilities and through community mental health providers can be highly effective.

Many service members are averse to taking medications, and you may be as well. For some, however, the first line of defense against panic attacks is medication. Ativan (lorazepam), for instance, is a short-acting medication frequently prescribed on an *as needed* (PRN) basis to panic sufferers. Taken during the first signs of a panic attack, it can quickly calm the mind and relax the body. For some, simply knowing that they have a couple pills on hand makes it easier for them to be out in the world. For those who are not comfortable with or whose military assignments do not allow this particular form of medication, there are alternatives. Remember that for many service members, the humiliation of having a panic attack in a public place may feel even worse than the attack itself. If your service member is suffering from panic attacks, consider speaking with him or her about having a health care provider—one with whom he or she feels comfortable—prescribe medication.

Preventing future panic attacks. Just as slow breathing can help your service member manage a panic attack once it has started, regular practice of slow breathing exercises can help him or her nip a panic attack in the bud and eventually prevent future panic attacks. You too may find benefit from slow breathing as a strategy for managing your stress and improving your overall health. You will find a slow breathing exercise in chapter 7.

Post-Traumatic Stress

My husband, a [veteran], has PTSD. I know my son has it too. Since Dad will not seek counseling, my son won't either. If Dad can handle PTSD without help, so can he. My daughter and I have my husband about 90% convinced to seek counseling. I'm praying once my husband seeks counseling, my son will too. (Tamara)

Any overwhelming or uncontrollable experience can constitute a traumatic event. Such events can happen to anyone at any age. A traumatic event may be a life-threatening experience or may involve witnessing something that elicits horror, intense fear, or a profound feeling of helplessness. Although not everyone deployed to a danger zone is exposed to traumatic events, there is a good likelihood that your service member experienced at least one traumatic event during deployment.

Different people can have different reactions to the same traumatic event. These reactions, which may begin immediately after the event or may not appear until months or in some cases years later, may have a mild to severe impact on a person's life. People who have experienced previous traumatic events may be particularly vulnerable to having a strong reaction to a subsequent traumatic event. Service members who experience multiple traumatic events during deployment or across several deployments may develop post-traumatic stress in reaction to their accumulated experiences rather than any one particular incident. Some of the more typical traumatic stress reactions are:

- Nightmares or unwanted waking images of the event
- Distress or upset when reminded of the event
- Avoidance of thoughts or reminders of the event
- Social withdrawal or difficulty feeling close to others
- Numb or flat emotions
- Impaired memory and concentration
- Sleep difficulties
- Anger or irritability
- Jumpiness
- Hypervigilance

When someone suffers from post-traumatic stress, the most important thing for him or her to understand is that *it's over.* For example, while it's true that your daughter with post-traumatic stress understands in a rational and practical sense that her last deployment is over—even if she is anxiously awaiting the next deployment—the primary problem is that her body and mind remain on "red alert" and she reacts to reminders and memories of the traumatic event as though it were still happening NOW. This means that the best way to help your daughter is to remind her that she is safe—that being stateside is not the same as being in a war zone—and to provide her the opportunity to process the traumatic experiences that plague her.

The power of processing. Unfortunately, rather than processing or working through traumatic memories, people with post-traumatic stress are driven to avoid them because of the discomfort if not terror that they can bring. While that's understandable, this avoidance actually powers post-traumatic stress because avoiding traumatic memories and reminders reinforces the idea that they are dangerous. This means that talking about traumatic memories, particularly with supportive loved ones like you, can be powerful medicine for your service member. But in addition to fear of his or her own reaction to the memories, the idea of talking about traumatic deployment experiences may cause your service member to worry that you will be burdened or overwhelmed by these stories or ashamed or judgmental of the things he or she has done. Or perhaps you won't understand or will unknowingly respond in a way that will upset him or her even more.

Please note that if your service member is in danger of harming himself or herself or others, has hallucinations, or is highly dissociative (tends to have intense flashbacks or to lose track of time and place), it's best that any processing of traumatic deployment events occur under the care of a mental health provider.

The act of asking. Maybe you would like to open the door for your son to begin processing his traumatic war experiences. By asking about his experiences, you send a powerful message that you as a member of his support system are willing to hear what he's been through. Even if he chooses to talk to other family members or friends, your reaching out to him may facilitate his reaching out to others. In fact, even if he chooses to talk with a therapist about his experiences there will be a role for you and his support system to play in his recovery.

If you do choose to invite your service member to talk, here is an example of how you might open that door: **"I understand that you experienced some things during your deployment that were very disturbing or upsetting and that these experiences continue to affect you today. I know that these experiences are difficult to think about, let alone talk about, but in order to move forward you need to find a way to talk about these memories so that they no longer interfere with your life. If you would like to share these memories with me now or at some point, I would be honored to listen."** Don't be surprised if you aren't immediately taken up on your offer. You may be turned down flat with "It's none of your business!" or more politely dismissed with "Maybe later." If your offer is rejected, try giving it some time and asking again when your service member seems in a more receptive mood.

If your service member appears open to the idea of talking with you about his or her experience, follow up by asking whether he or she has any concerns about taking this step. Show your service member that you respect his or her concerns by outlining a plan for the conversation together. This plan should include:

- A place for the conversation where your service member feels safe and comfortable

- A time for the conversation that does not fall just before or after a commitment and is free from distractions such as phone calls, e-mails, texts, friends, or family members

- A *maximum* time frame for the conversation

  For example, don't allow your daughter's processing to go on all night long. It's not necessary and may even be overwhelming for her to "get it all out" in one telling, particularly if she experienced a number of traumatic events. Two hours tends to be a reasonable maximum, but you and your service member may decide to make it shorter.

- A *minimum* time frame for the conversation

  While you don't want your service member to become flooded by his or her experience, it's important that your service member not try to escape the situation before his or her anxiety has peaked, as doing so reinforces the idea that the memories are dangerous. Setting a minimum time frame of thirty to forty-five minutes will help prevent this from happening.

- A "cool down" routine

  Have a plan for what to do if your service member becomes highly agitated or angered while telling his or her story. This can include relaxing activities, such as slow breathing or taking a short walk, or having a snack (see chapter 7 for more details). *If your service member is prone to angry outbursts that cause you to feel threatened (see "Anger" above), it's best that he or she learns to manage that anger before you help process the trauma.*

- How your service member would like you to respond during the conversation
  - Would your service member prefer physical contact or not?
  - Would your service member like you to comment, ask questions, or remain silent?

- A "wrap up" or reward plan

  Maybe you and your service member can watch a funny movie, go out and enjoy dinner, take a walk, or shoot some hoops. Think of something that you enjoy doing together that will be relaxing and rewarding after the conversation has ended.

There are times when service members need extra support to process their traumatic events. It may make sense to find a mental health professional if talking about the event leads to any of the following:

- An increase in dangerous thinking (i.e., your service member has thoughts of self-harm or of harming others)
- An increase in alcohol or drug use
- An increase in angry outbursts
- Panic attacks
- Problems in *your* emotional health (e.g., an increase in your substance use, anger, sleep problems, relationship problems)

While a moderate increase in symptoms is common initially, a significant increase may mean that the work that needs to be accomplished is best done with the guidance of a mental health professional. If you're unsure whether your service member is ready to talk with you about his or her experiences, or if you believe professional support is needed, please turn to chapter 5 to learn more about how to find and access mental health services.

An additional tool for learning about post-traumatic stress is the mobile app PTSD Coach, which provides information on symptoms, stress management skills, treatment, and resources. You and your service member may benefit from this easy-to-use app (www.ptsd.va.gov/public/pages/PTSDCoach.asp).

Taking Care of Yourself

My son has shared some of the atrocities of war with us. He has kicked in many a door, and he has nightmares that someone is kicking in the door to our house and having us go through the same trauma that he beset on others. (Maggie)

It can be difficult to hear your service member talk about times when he or she was under threat or witnessed horrific events. Listening to your service member tell about such experiences may bring up a great deal of emotions including fear, anger, grief, and helplessness. Don't feel as if you need to completely hide your emotions—it's normal to shed tears in the presence of your son or daughter's pain—however, it's important that you take care of yourself during this process. Be sure to practice the self-care strategies in chapter 7 and to pay close attention to your own stress level. If you have experienced trauma yourself, your service member's story may trigger your own distressing memories that need to be processed as well. Consider whether you are prepared to support your service member in this way. If not, that's okay—there are plenty of other ways for you to help.

If Your Service Member Has Been Sexually Assaulted

One of the most difficult things for any parent to learn of is that their son or daughter has been sexually assaulted. When sexual assault occurs during military service, such news can be absolutely devastating. Military personnel are obviously trained to face certain threats inherent in military service, particularly during deployment, but they are not trained to face the potential threat of forcible rape or other nonconsensual sexual acts, and parents are often at a loss as to how to understand these incidents and support their service member.

Unfortunately most sexual harassment or sexual assault of service members, whether during deployment or stateside, is perpetrated by other service members. While females are much more commonly targeted, male-on-male sexual assault does happen and can be extremely emotionally injurious.

As with civilian sexual assaults, the situations that lead up to an attack vary greatly. It's also common for both civilian and military survivors to keep silent about their assault, though in the military, the fear of retaliation, weakness, and blame is generally much stronger.

In the military, survivors of sexual assault are often afterward repeatedly exposed to their attackers, since survivor and perpetrator are generally stationed on the same military base, fort, post, or ship. This can lead to a general distrust of fellow service members that is truly devastating, especially when the sexual assault happens during a deployment, given the interdependence necessary to maintain the safety of each individual and each unit as a whole. If the survivor does report the incident while in the theater of operations, how the situation is actually handled can be very complicated—particularly in a remote location—despite established reporting guidelines and procedures.

As a result of these challenges and of the assault itself, your service member may feel depressed or anxious. You may notice behaviors such as needing to be in control, social isolation, increased substance abuse, difficulty sleeping, or "catastrophic thinking" (dwelling on the "worst-case scenario").

You, too, will have your own reactions when you hear the news that your service member was sexually assaulted. Anger or even rage at the perpetrator and the military are common responses. If you have served in the military yourself, your perspective on your own military service may change. In addition, you may feel guilty for not better protecting your son or daughter and have thoughts like *Why did I let him enlist?* If you are also a survivor of sexual abuse, assault, or rape, you may have an added sensitivity to the changes that take place within a person after these types of violent events. In chapter 7 we discuss how to develop and use your own set of coping strategies in order to ensure that you can be an effective support to your service member, especially after hearing such distressing details.

But how do you approach your service member about his or her experience in a concerned way that doesn't initiate a defensive reaction? This is not easy. However, one thing to consider is the sense of isolation and guilt that often accompanies having been raped, molested, or significantly harassed while in the military. Reach out in a manner that (1) communicates your willingness to hear what happened without judgment; (2) allows your service member to tell you when he or she is ready to talk; and (3) includes patience and compassion for the multitude of emotions associated with sharing the experience (e.g., fear of rejection by you, fear of being blamed for the assault or harassment, anger and sadness about having been victimized).

Realistically, unless your service member or someone else reported the assault, you may not learn about it for many years. Sifting through the changes you may notice within your son or daughter after deployment to differentiate between those brought on by war experiences and those possibly brought on by sexual assault is difficult. Being patient and periodically telling your service member that you would like to be a supportive resource may not seem like much, but this just may be the key gesture that makes possible his or her eventual recovery.

An important reminder: If you are concerned that your son or daughter may have thoughts of suicide or self-harm, please turn to the section "Thoughts of Suicide" at the end of this chapter.

Depression

While post-traumatic stress is strictly caused by a traumatic event or events, a service member might develop post-deployment depression for a wide variety of reasons. These include:

- Disabling or disfiguring physical injuries
- Guilt or grief
- Difficulties readjusting to base or civilian life
- Dissatisfaction with life following deployment (e.g., being passed over for promotion, being underemployed)
- Home-front stressors or losses experienced during or after deployment (e.g., divorce, financial struggles, unemployment)
- Other associated psychological injuries such as post-traumatic stress

Most people think they understand what it means to be depressed. Just as everyone has experienced worry at one time or another, we all know what it is to feel sad or blue. But depression, unlike normal sadness, is a psychological injury. More than just a brief period of feeling down, it's like being stuck in a dark hole with no hope to light your way. Depression usually lasts longer than normal sadness and doesn't resolve on its own.

Although you may have clearly noted that your service member has experienced one or more of the potential causes of post-deployment depression, you may not be sure whether he or she is truly depressed. This is because depression wears a number of faces that can be particularly difficult to discern among members of the military culture, in which emotional restraint is the norm and great pains are taken to deny or hide perceived weakness.

The Many Faces of Depression

"I'm just so pissed off lately I don't even want to leave the house," Chuck, an Iraq veteran, told his mother, Ann, on the phone. "Not even to play basketball? You love basketball," said Ann hopefully. "Nah—the only thing I want to do is lie on the couch and watch TV. It's like I don't have the energy to do anything anymore." "Maybe you're depressed." "Are you kidding? It's not like I'm lying here cryin' my eyes out! I just don't feel like seeing anybody or doing anything. Who needs it?"

Ann guessed that her son, who was otherwise physically healthy, might be suffering from depression. That's because unlike Chuck, she understood that depression was not just the TV version—someone lying in a dark room "cryin' their eyes out"—and that among military professionals like her son, depression might take the form of irritability, exhaustion, or even flu-like symptoms. Ann also saw other signs of depression in Chuck such as lack of interest in things he used to enjoy, isolation, and negativity.

While Chuck was experiencing fatigue, some suffering from depression may be tense and unable to sleep. Instead of deep sadness or irritability, others feel simply numb and may describe a sense of emptiness that they can't quite explain. Regardless of which face it wears, depression can be debilitating, stifling a person's ability to thrive in everyday life.

How You Can Help

As complicated as depression may be to spot, its roots are actually quite simple. Depression is really just a combination of *inactivity* and *negative thinking*. That should make it quite easy to help your service member overcome depression—right? Well, not exactly. The problem is that inactivity and negative thinking have a way of intertwining and spiraling down like a drilling rig, digging deeper and deeper. The less people with depression do, the more negatively they think about themselves and their world; the more negatively they think, the less they do. What this means is that in order to help, you need to first encourage your service member to engage in activities even when he or she doesn't feel like it. And make no mistake—he or she *won't* feel like it. But as most parents know, while it may be difficult, it's worthwhile to push your children to do things they don't want to do. Bear in mind that your daughter, for example, still may not enjoy an activity even as she's doing it, but just keep nudging because *the more she does, the more she does*, and after a time she'll have that "hole" filled in with activities, hope, and newfound energy.

It's important to note that if your service member suffers from chronic depression lasting for more than a few months, or severe depressive symptoms that haven't responded to the support and interventions that you and other loved ones have provided or to any strategies attempted on his or her own, he or she may require antidepressant medication in combination with formal counseling or therapy. Encourage your service member to see a health care provider, and refer to chapter 5 for tips on accessing mental health services. Above all, if you are at all concerned that the depression is at a point where your service member is contemplating self-harm, turn straight to the end of this chapter to read "Thoughts of Suicide," and do not hesitate to dial 911 if you believe your service member is in immediate danger.

A Note on Coping Strategies

There are a variety of coping strategies that you can apply not only to the support and care of your service member, but to yourself as well. These include:

- Healthy behaviors such as exercise, good diet, and sleep management
- Relaxation strategies such as slow breathing, yoga, and meditation
- Antianxiety and antidepressant medications
- Therapy or counseling

We'll discuss coping strategies like these in greater detail in chapter 7.

While *you* may see the value in these kinds of strategies, it may be difficult to convince your service member to consider them. Here's a good way to address resistance: **"I understand that you are hesitant to try ______________. Maybe you think it's silly or that you're doing just fine without it. But over the past ____ months/years, I've seen you struggle with (name injury or give examples) and it seems that you could benefit from another strategy or two to help you move forward."** Be sure to ask your service member whether he or she has any specific concerns about the particular strategy you're suggesting. If you're unable to answer such questions right away, say that you'll look into it and get back to him or her. Above all, don't give up. You may need to have this conversation a few times before your service member agrees to try something new. You might even offer to join him or her—whether it be in exercise, therapy, or yoga, you could find yourself feeling healthier too!

Struggles of the Spirit

> *...[s]he told me there might be something to Angels and the God I believe in, because even though she had close calls, she and [her] unit were still safe and she told me to keep praying.* (Daniela)

In addition to physical and psychological injuries that may result, deployment experiences can shake if not devastate some service members' moral and spiritual beliefs. Your service member may seriously question his or her sense of self and the world in light of recent experiences. You may find your own faith or belief system similarly challenged after hearing about some of those experiences or witnessing your service member's struggles. Below we'll discuss such moral and spiritual challenges and offer specific strategies to help both you and your service member consider and discuss any struggles or shifts that deployment may have provoked.

Moral Struggles

As different as people may be from one another in race, education, and family environment, by and large they develop similar fundamental beliefs about the way the world works. They tend to believe, for instance, that good things happen to good people and bad things happen to bad people; that things happen for a reason; that their loved ones are generally safe, even when they're not around; and that children outlive their parents (Janoff-Bulman 2002).

But something like combat or exposure to deployment-related trauma has a way of bending and in some cases altering those beliefs, both for those who serve and for the families who anxiously await their return. Some service members return from deployment affected by a pervasive distrust. Instead of feeling relatively safe in the world as they had prior to deployment, they now believe that they must be prepared for danger at all times. Rather than valuing close relationships, they now have difficulty trusting even their own family members. (For those who believed even before they deployed that the world is an unsafe place, that nobody can be trusted, or that things happen for no reason, deployment-related trauma can reinforce this negative view.)

Deployment may also deeply affect service members' beliefs about their country and the military. During deployment, military personnel may witness events that cause them to question their country's presence or purpose in a foreign land. Or decisions made by superiors may lead them to question the authority and military structure that they used to respect.

Identity Struggles

In addition to beliefs about the world, deployment can also shape service members' beliefs about themselves. Before deploying, many service members see themselves as good and moral; strong and capable; responsible and in control. For some, deployment actually strengthens these beliefs. But others who experience trauma or tragic loss may return with the sense that they're weak, unable to control their fate, or doomed to failure. And some, rather than good and moral, now see themselves as bad or even evil.

Those who return with their self-image intact may still struggle. For example, your son may be challenged or even insulted by those who disagreed with our leaders' decision to go to war, causing him to question his patriotism. Or your daughter may be disrespected by those who still believe that women don't carry guns or supervise troops, leading her to question her very profession.

Spiritual Struggles

While deployment strengthens some service members' belief in a higher power, it causes others to question their own faith. They may ask how their higher power could allow such violence and suffering. They may doubt that their higher power could continue to love them after all that they have done and may even believe that they can never set foot in a place of worship again.

Existential Struggles

Finally, the experience of deployment, particularly to a war zone, can be so profound that it makes people question their very existence. Your son, for example, may be struggling with the great questions of who he is and why he's here—the purpose and meaning of life itself. These are of course natural questions to ask when you are in your twenties and still struggling to "make sense of it all." But when that normal developmental period of soul-searching and identity-seeking is disrupted by combat or deployment trauma, such questions can become difficult to bear—even overwhelming.

Signs and Symptoms

So how do you know whether your service member's beliefs have been shaken or maybe even altered by deployment? How do you know whether he or she is struggling to make sense of senseless events? Here are a few signs:

- Sudden departure from the military
- Uncharacteristic irresponsibility at work or home
- Conflicts with authority
- Withdrawal from or distrust of friends or family
- No longer going to a customary place of worship
- Repeated comments about the meaninglessness of life
- Repeated self-deprecating remarks

Guilt and Shame

He was transferred to another base with another guy from his prior post. They were the same rank. He and my son were up for the same position when they arrived, and my son really wanted the position....

> *the other guy got the position and my son told me, "I wanted to kick him in the knee!" Within the first two months of the deployment, the other guy stepped on an IED and lost both legs and a significant part of one arm. That haunts my son and he still recalls saying, "I want to kick him in the knee." I know he is asking the $64 million question of why wasn't it me.* (Clay)

Returning service members wrestle with internal struggles that may have their roots in guilt or shame or some combination of both. Although the terms "guilt" and "shame" are often used interchangeably, guilt is the more concrete term, referring to something an individual did or neglected to do that he or she believes is responsible for a negative outcome. It's guilt that causes people to say "I should have" or "I shouldn't have." Shame, on the other hand, is a pervasive negative sense of self: "I'm a failure"; "I'm weak." Often, feelings of guilt can build to shame. For instance, someone who believes that she should have prevented something bad from happening may generalize this belief into a shameful sense of failure. It's important to recognize when your service member is suffering from guilt or shame, because either of these may underlie depression or post-traumatic stress.

To know whether your service member is experiencing guilt or shame, start by listening for the "shoulds" and "shouldn'ts" along with any negative self-labels. Once you've identified these statements, begin to help your service member challenge them. Point out that the "shoulds" of guilt are generally the result of viewing past events from the safety and security of the present. Imagining how things might have gone better, perhaps your service member fails to realize the realistic limitations and pressures he or she faced—his or her judgment may have been clouded by stress or fatigue. Perhaps your service member had to make a split-second decision or was simply following orders. Whatever the case, your service member most likely did the best he or she possibly could under the circumstances. Help your service member turn "should" statements into *wishes*, replacing "I *should* have prevented it from happening" with "I *wish* I could have prevented it from happening." Challenge shame statements by pointing out examples that contradict the label; for example, when your son refers to himself as a failure, recall and recount his successes. Point out proud examples of his strength and courage that help challenge or contradict statements of weakness.

As with the processing of your service member's trauma, you may or may not be the best person for this task. Perhaps it would be most helpful to identify someone in your community—a priest, rabbi, or minister and/or a mental health professional—who can facilitate these conversations.

Conclusion

Deployment can have a profound and varied impact on service members and their loved ones. While touched by these events, most members of the military community are eventually able to move forward with their lives. Some, however, suffer in silence from psychological injuries like depression, post-traumatic stress, or panic attacks. Others wrestle with challenged beliefs or with guilt or shame—often in combination with psychological injuries. You can help your service member overcome these "invisible wounds" by collaborating on effective strategies or by strongly encouraging him or her to explore treatment options. Don't let the military mind-set block your service member's road to recovery. Make restoration of your son or daughter's well-being, in addition to your own, a real priority with tangible goals.

Chapter Tips

- One of the most important things you can do as a parent is simply *understand.* First, recognize that your service member's unusual, hurtful, or even destructive behaviors may be indicative of a psychological injury that occurred during deployment. Second, learn the signs and symptoms of such injuries so that you can identify the problem and offer the most effective support.

- Even though your service member's behavior may be symptomatic of a psychological injury, it's important to set limits when things start to get out of control.

- Your service member may be bothered by distressing memories that he or she is trying hard to avoid. Consider giving your son or daughter the opportunity to talk about these experiences in a way that helps him or her feel safe and supported. Open the door.

- Your service member may deny his or her injuries and resist your help at every turn. Yet even seemingly small victories like getting your service member to join you at the gym or on a long walk can be an important step toward recovering. Stay positive and don't give up!

- For some suggested sources of further information and support, turn to the list of resources at the back of the book.

Thoughts of Suicide

If you believe that your son or daughter is currently in danger of harming or killing himself or herself, CALL 911 IMMEDIATELY.

The pain of physical, psychological, and/or moral injuries may at times become so great that it leads service members to think about harming or killing themselves. These thoughts can range from wishing that they would die in their sleep or have a fatal accident, to impulsively driving toward oncoming traffic only to veer away at the last second, to carefully planning suicide. Most service members will not readily admit that they are having these thoughts but may show some of the following signs of suicidal thinking:

- Unusual withdrawal from friends, family members, or work duties

- Neglecting to take care of themselves (e.g., not eating, not bathing, not changing clothes)

- Expressing hopelessness or desperation (e.g., "I'm never going to be okay"; "There's no way out of this"; "There's no point in trying anymore")
- Expressions of intense or overwhelming guilt, grief, burdensomeness, or shame (e.g., "I should have died instead of him"; "I'll never be able to forgive myself for what I've done"; "You'd be better off without me")
- Unusual risk-taking behavior or participating in dangerous activities (e.g., high-speed motorcycle riding or unsafe driving)
- Giving away prized possessions or suddenly putting affairs in order
- Attempts to access weapons, pills, or other means of self-harm, or refusal to relinquish weapons or other dangerous possessions

If you are concerned that your service member may be having thoughts of self-harm, DO NOT HESITATE TO ASK HIM OR HER DIRECTLY. Asking will *not* put a thought into your service member's head that he or she hasn't already had, and you may just save your child's life.

Further support and information is available for both you and your service member at:

The Veterans Crisis Line
1-800-273-8255 (Press "1")
veteranscrisisline.net

---

chapter 4

Deployment's Toll on the Body: Physical Injuries

People don't realize how battered soldiers' bodies are by mission after mission, up and down mountains in unbearable weather conditions. It takes a big toll on the physical side, as well as the mental side. (Lisa)

On May 28, 2012, CNN reported that more than 480,000 US troops had been wounded in action in Iraq and Afghanistan since 2003. While the media has provided such statistics time and again, especially on national holidays like Memorial Day, the vast majority of Americans have enjoyed their lives and holiday barbecues untouched by the challenges faced by our nation's wounded heroes. However, for parents like you who are keenly aware that each casualty is someone's son or daughter, these statistics hit home intensely, even after deployment.

Over the past decade, a small but significant number of service members have returned from deployment with serious physical injuries, including moderate to severe traumatic brain injury (TBI), amputations, and spinal cord injuries. These individuals often face prolonged hospitalizations and rehabilitation. Not as public but still significant are the tens of thousands of military personnel who return with physical injuries—such as mild TBI, knee pain, back pain, or tinnitus ("ringing" in one or both ears)—that are less serious but may cause chronic problems and interfere with their lives.

We have written this chapter to familiarize you with common physical injuries sustained during deployment because military personnel often minimize their injuries, preferring not to disclose any pain or discomfort. Since some of these conditions, such as mild TBI and musculoskeletal injuries, are difficult to detect and diagnose, it's our hope that you can use this information along with the practical strategies we present to team up with your service member to get the most effective help. We also understand that it's extremely difficult for parents to see their child suffer. In this chapter, we'll speak to the emotional toll of service members' physical injuries, on them as well as on those who love them.

Common Physical Injuries

Over the past decade, there has been a tidal wave of service members returning from deployment with operational stress injuries related to "the wear and tear of accumulated stress" (Nash 2007, 57). While common, these injuries can be painful and worrisome. In this section, we'll focus on musculoskeletal injuries and related pain, mild TBI, and tinnitus.

Musculoskeletal Injuries

She was out in the heat and dirt moving 100-pound packages on and off trucks. She WORKED!!! (Derek)

The most common health issue in combat veterans who have returned from Iraq and Afghanistan is musculoskeletal injury with chronic pain (Spelman et al. 2012). These injuries, which involve muscles, joints, cartilage, tendons, ligaments, and other connective tissue, can significantly affect a person's stability and movement and interfere with everyday functioning. They can result from daily repetitive strain, heavy lifting, or trauma to a particular body region caused by falls, sudden jerky movements, sprains, or dislocations. For service members, these injuries most often occur to the back, knee, or shoulder and are related to the physical demands and stresses placed on them during training and deployment. Physical stresses such as transporting heavy body armor, weapons, and supply packs and trekking through harsh environs and temperatures can lead to acute injuries as well as wear and tear. In addition, those deployed to underdeveloped regions may develop injuries from repeated driving over rough terrain, while those deployed to war zones may be injured by blasts.

Pain

My daughter now has a serious back problem from carrying heavy equipment. Walking on steel for years has also affected her feet.
(Peter)

Although it may resolve without significant long-term consequences, pain caused by musculoskeletal injuries can still be quite challenging in the short term. For many, though, this pain is long-lasting or chronic, and it can take a real toll both physically and psychologically, diminishing their ability to enjoy family events, concentrate at work, perform household tasks, or do other everyday things.

If you've experienced any extended period of pain yourself, you know that it can negatively color a person's mood and outlook on life. Mental health conditions like depression or post-traumatic stress that can persist in concert with pain often exacerbate it, creating a vicious circle in which pain and psychological reactions trigger each other. This is *not* to say that pain is "all in your head." While pain can influence a person's attitude and perceptions, it is—simply put—a reaction to an injury or disease. In our work with veterans from various eras, we have seen numerous examples of chronic pain caused by injuries sustained during military service. Some of these veterans have experienced only intermittent "flare-ups" of pain, while others have lived with daily discomfort that is at times excruciating. The factors that determine the frequency and level of pain are quite complex, and modern-day assessments and treatments reflect this complexity. The more you and your service member understand pain, the better able your service member will be to manage it. In an effort to increase awareness and understanding of the issues facing those with chronic pain, a number of organizations have created educational websites, some of which we have listed in the resources at the back of the book, under "Physical Health."

Pain Assessment

Untreated pain can significantly interfere with a person's life, leading to depression, inactivity, and a potential worsening of the injury. But pain-causing musculoskeletal injuries are often difficult to detect. Even if an X-ray or MRI proves your son or daughter has a service-related injury such as a herniated disc or torn rotator cuff, the "suck it up" philosophy that permeates military culture may be preventing him or her from admitting to the pain and getting the needed help. It's important that your service member be able to acknowledge and discuss any pain that he or she experiences. If you're wondering whether your service member is suffering from undisclosed pain, here are some signs to look for:

- Objective evidence such as facial tension (clenched teeth, furrowed brow, or grimacing); uncharacteristic gasping or groaning during physical activities; or caution when sitting, bending, or walking
- Avoidance of any of the following: lifting, stairs, steep inclines, previously enjoyed physical activities, or extended car trips
- Disturbed sleep
- Extensive use of over-the-counter medications such as aspirin, ibuprofen, or sleep aids
- Increased alcohol use
- Depression, irritability, or social withdrawal

Once you've determined that your service member may be suffering from pain, the next step is to raise your concerns. How you go about this depends primarily on your relationship and level of communication with your service member. You may determine, for instance, that the concerns you have would be better received if they came from another family member or a friend. Regardless of who broaches the subject, the best approach is to first acknowledge your service member's tendency to "suck it up," then offer concrete evidence for your concerns with statements such as **"I know that you don't like to complain, and I respect your strength and courage, but I've noticed that you have been __________ (e.g., avoiding stairs) since returning from deployment, and I'm concerned that you're experiencing pain that is interfering with your life."**

While your service member may admit to some pain, he or she will probably be quick to add, "I'm fine" or "It's not that bad." Even so, you can encourage him or her to see a health care provider, "just to be sure." In the end, if your service member agrees to see a health care provider simply to make *you* feel better, that's perfectly fine so long as it gets him or her in the door. Be sure to have names and numbers of health care providers at the ready so that you can strike while the iron is hot. What *type* of provider your service member sees initially is less important than your service member's level of comfort with and trust in this person. For example, your daughter may be initially reticent to go to a VHA facility. Further, she may be more comfortable with female providers than male ones or prefer to see a trusted family doctor rather than a specialist. So long as the provider is able to make an initial assessment followed by appropriate referrals, what matters most is that your service member be able to talk honestly about the pain. Turn to chapter 5 for a more detailed discussion of the importance of trust in and comfort with health care providers.

Tracking the Pain

Again, because pain is best measured by self-report, your service member will be asked a number of questions by each professional involved in his or her treatment. The effectiveness of any treatment plan hinges on the patient's ability to identify and communicate the status of his or her pain level and functioning. It's therefore recommended that your service member start a "Pain Diary" and/or "Pain Management Log" as soon as possible. Pain logs and diaries are used to track multiple variables including activities, therapies, and medications; pain-related sleep disturbance; and the frequency, intensity, and location of pain. If your service member is seen in a pain clinic or by a pain management specialist, he or she will most likely be provided with forms for tracking pain. There are also a variety of templates available online through Partners Against Pain (partnersagainstpain.com) and the American Chronic Pain Association (theacpa.org/Pain-Management-Tools.aspx) as well as "My Pain Diary," an app available through iTunes. There will undoubtedly be times that your service member does not feel like filling out pain-tracking forms. Try to encourage your service member during these times by reminding him or her that the more information providers have on their patients, the better able they are to assist them in managing their pain.

Pain Management—It's a Team Effort

Because chronic pain affects and is affected by a variety of systems and factors, it's ideally managed using a combination of treatments provided through a team approach. According to the American Chronic Pain Association (2012b), in order to regain control of their lives, chronic pain sufferers must make the move from "patient" to "person" to become active participants in their multidisciplinary treatment team, which can include physicians and nurses, occupational and physical therapists, mental health and vocational counselors, pharmacists, and nutritionists, as well as significant others such as parents, partner (e.g., spouse), and close friends. Because service members with chronic pain tend to require ongoing care from multiple providers, it's important to consider support staff, such as receptionists and transportation services, as integral members of the team as well.

Ideally, the entire treatment team works together within a single setting such as a pain clinic or center. Many VHA Medical Centers have pain clinics, as do most teaching hospitals and major medical facilities. If you do not have access to a multidisciplinary pain clinic or if your service member is seeking services outside of his or her primary clinic, it's imperative that the providers involved maintain regular communication with each other regarding assessments, services, and medications. A chiropractor or massage therapist not working with the team, for instance, can unwittingly undo months of physical therapy by addressing an injury in an alternate and opposing manner. Even more concerning are the medication errors and abuses that can occur when a pain sufferer receives prescriptions through multiple providers. We'll now turn to this and other medication issues.

Medication Management

Generally, when people think of pain management they think of medication. Yet while analgesics (pain relievers) are the most common treatment for pain, there is no such thing as a magic pill, and "partial relief" is the most realistic expectation when taking medications (ACPA 2012a, 10). Determining the type, dosage, and (when appropriate) combination of medications to address pain is a complicated and sometimes frustrating process in which each patient's response to medication is unique. Personal circumstances and preferences (e.g., responsibilities, lifestyle, health care coverage, financial circumstances) should be considered when medication is being prescribed. If your service member is prescribed a pain medication, it's therefore important that he or she ask the provider to fully explain the benefits and potential side effects beforehand, not just blindly take it "as the doctor ordered." Better yet, your service member can create and keep a list of specific questions to ask. Here are some examples of questions that may be pertinent to your service member's situation:

- "Will I be able to drive on this medication?"
- "Can it affect my focus, memory, or concentration?"
- "Can it make me irritable or depressed?"
- "Can it upset my stomach?"

- "Can it disturb my sleep or make me drowsy?"
- "What does it cost, and is there a generic or lower-cost alternative?"
- "What are the possible interactions between this medication and the others that I am currently taking?"
- "Can this medication become addictive?"

If your service member still has questions after talking with a health care provider, he or she may find it helpful to speak with a pharmacist. Nowadays, many people go online to research the medications they've been prescribed. More often than not, however, they find complaints and horror stories that do not accurately reflect the actual odds of a particular reaction to a medication. If your service member plans to search for information online, he or she should ask his or her health care provider or treatment team to suggest reputable websites. Even drug labels should be read with the understanding that pharmaceutical companies are required to list every *possible* side effect, and the fact that a side effect *can* happen does not mean that it *will*.

As the saying goes, you don't know whether something will work until you try it. And even if a medication doesn't work as well *as hoped*, it still may be worth taking. According to the American Chronic Pain Association, as regards medication, "benefit is suggested when there is a significant increase in the person's level of functioning, a reduction or elimination of pain complaints, [and] a more positive and hopeful attitude and when side effects are minimal or controllable" (ACPA 2012a, 27). If your service member decides to try a particular medication, it's important that he or she track any negative reactions as well as any changes in pain or functioning (see "Tracking the Pain," above). If unpleasant side effects in the first few days are minor, such as dizziness or stomach upset, he or she may want to try to "stick it out" to see whether the benefits outweigh the discomfort, because sometimes these side effects wear off or become more tolerable. If they do not, or if the side effects are serious (e.g., vomiting or chest pains), he or she should contact a health care provider immediately.

Abuse and disuse. Because of the high risk for abuse of painkillers like Vicodin (hydrocodone) or OxyContin (oxycodone), if your service member has been prescribed these medications, be aware that they should be used cautiously and only as prescribed. Unfortunately, people with conditions such as insomnia may misuse and abuse pain medications even when more effective treatments are available. Some people use painkillers to self-medicate mental health conditions like post-traumatic stress in an effort to block out painful memories and reduce emotional pain, which can actually worsen both physical and emotional suffering. If your service member has a history of alcohol or drug abuse, he or she should discuss this with the prescribing health care provider in order to ensure that medications are properly monitored and managed. When taking any prescription pain medication, it's best to abstain from alcohol use. The combination of alcohol and painkillers can be detrimental if not deadly.

Although some service members are at risk for medication abuse, others suffer the consequences of medication *disuse*. For some, the mere thought of taking a prescription medication makes them feel weak, as though it's a sign that they are disabled and in need of a "crutch" just to get through the day. Others may avoid any medication that they see as addictive, even if they have no history of or tendency toward addictive behavior. Still, these service members often don't express their reservations and willingly accept a prescription knowing that they have no intention of ever filling it. Or they may fill the prescription but then take the medication only when their pain becomes extreme. This "chasing the pain" can actually lead to periodic overuse of medications, while inadequate pain management can interfere with daily functioning and potentially worsen the injury.

Still other service members may attempt to address their pain on their own through over-the-counter (OTC) medications such as NSAIDS (nonsteroidal anti-inflammatory drugs, which can also be by prescription), aspirin, and acetaminophen. These medications, which can be helpful and appropriate for occasional treatment of minor or acute pain, should be carefully considered and managed when addressing chronic pain. While OTC medications do not pose the same risk of addiction as prescription painkillers, long-term use can have significant health consequences including gastrointestinal, cardiovascular, liver, and kidney damage (President & Fellows of Harvard College 2000–2006). It's also quite possible that prescription medications would provide greater relief, leading to improved functioning and healing. Regardless, any medications, whether OTC or prescription, should be made known to the entire treatment team and considered as part of the overall treatment plan.

Integrative Care

Integrative medicine combines mainstream Western medicine with complementary and alternative medicine (CAM) approaches such as biofeedback, acupuncture, yoga, and massage therapy. In terms of philosophy, integrative care programs use a holistic approach to healing, with attention to the mind, body, and spirit of each individual. Since the late 1980s, numerous research studies and scientific papers have pointed toward the effectiveness of alternative and integrative treatments. As alternatives to Western medicine have been popularized by well-known authors such as Andrew Weil, MD, they have made their way into the pain management field. One of the more popular and accessible of these interventions is the mindfulness-based approach, in which the connection between mind and body is used to change the way that people perceive and process pain. Jon Kabat-Zinn, PhD, the pioneer of this approach and founding executive director of the Center for Mindfulness in Medicine, Health Care, and Society at the University of Massachusetts Medical School, has scientifically demonstrated the effectiveness of mindfulness techniques. He has produced a number of books and audio recordings for individuals suffering from pain, including *Full Catastrophe Living: Using the Wisdom of Your Body and Mind to Face Stress, Pain, and Illness* (1990) and *Mindfulness Meditation for Pain Relief: Guided Practices for Reclaiming Your Body and Your Life* (2009).

Mindfulness-based treatment is just one example of the alternative approaches that can be integrated into traditional Western medicine to provide your service member with the most comprehensive range of pain management services. While some pain clinics offer a wide array of services including mindfulness training, acupuncture, and massage therapy, others are more narrowly focused on traditional methods. If the facility where your service member primarily receives care and services does not offer a particular treatment modality that you think may be helpful, do not hesitate to request a recommendation or referral and seek services outside of the clinic.

Traumatic Brain Injury (TBI)

He was hit by an IED and it was a never-ending 15 month deployment. (Melody)

The mother quoted above (Melody) probably couldn't stop worrying that her son had sustained a TBI. Hundreds of thousands of US troops have experienced one or more TBIs during deployment—many from explosions or other blasts. In simple terms, a TBI is "a blow or jolt to the head or a penetrating head injury that disrupts the normal function of the brain" (DVBIC 2012a, n.p.). Not all head injuries lead to TBI, however; there must be some change in the person's mental state—for example, disorientation, confusion, or unconsciousness for period of time, even if brief (DVBIC 2012c).

Although each TBI is different and can affect an individual in various ways, TBIs are divided into two main categories: *Open head* or penetrating injury is caused by a foreign object, such as a bullet or piece of shrapnel, entering the skull. *Closed head* or non-penetrating injury, on the other hand, is caused by external forces acting upon the brain but not actually penetrating the brain matter. This can result from something like a car accident or being hit by an object (CDC 2012). Non-penetrating TBI is classified as mild, moderate, or severe based on what happened at the time of the injury: how long the individual experienced an alteration in consciousness, loss of consciousness, or post-traumatic amnesia (any loss of memory for events immediately after the injury) (DVBIC 2012c; VA/DoD 2009). For instance, someone with mild TBI may have lost consciousness for only a few minutes, while someone with severe TBI may have suffered loss of consciousness and post-traumatic amnesia for several days, if not longer, and may also show findings on brain imaging. What is important to understand is that the severity or duration of symptoms (which we'll describe later) does not dictate the severity of the injury.

While deployment-related TBIs have received increased attention given the wars in Iraq and Afghanistan, approximately 1.7 million TBIs take place in the United States every year (Faul et al. 2010). As among civilians, the vast majority of TBIs among military personnel are mild. From 2000 until the second quarter of 2012, of the 253,330 medical diagnoses of TBI among US military personnel worldwide, 76.8 percent were mild, 16.6 percent were moderate, 1 percent were severe, 1.6 percent were penetrating, and 4 percent were not classifiable (DMSS, TMDS 2012). Of these military TBIs, 84 percent occurred in non-deployed settings and resulted from things like motor vehicle accidents, falls, sports, recreational activities, and training activities (DVBIC 2012b). So even though we focus on combat-related TBIs in this section, it's important to recognize that service members actually sustain more TBIs in garrison than on the battlefield.

Our discussion will focus on mild TBI, since it's the most common. According to the Defense and Veterans Brain Injury Center (DVBIC Working Group 2006), "Mild TBI in military operational settings is defined as an injury to the brain resulting from an external force and/or acceleration/deceleration mechanism from an event such as a blast, fall, direct impact, or motor vehicle accident, which causes an alteration in mental status that typically results in the temporally related onset of symptoms such as: headache, nausea, vomiting, dizziness/balance problems, fatigue, insomnia/sleep disturbances, drowsiness, sensitivity to light/ noise, blurred vision, difficulty remembering, and/or difficulty concentrating."

Basically, two conditions must be satisfied in order for a person to be diagnosed with a mild TBI. First, a traumatic event must have happened. Let's consider some examples:

- Charles was hit in the head by falling debris.
- Jenny was thrown back and hit her head on the pavement.
- Michael was riding in a Humvee when it rolled over.

- Chelsey was hit by a mortar blast.

Second, the person must have experienced a loss of consciousness or alteration of consciousness. Some with TBI describe this as having seen stars, feeling dazed or confused, or being knocked unconscious for some time.

You may have already known or guessed that mild TBI is actually the same as a concussion—the two terms are interchangeable (VA/DoD 2009). However, the main difference between, let's say, a sports concussion and a concussion sustained in combat is whether other injuries are sustained and what happens next. While most civilians who suffer a concussion recover very quickly, for service members who have been in a war zone, the trajectory of recovery is generally different, as they often have many other medical or psychological issues. And even those without other injuries who are able to remain in theater may continue to face many stressors such as sleep deprivation, poor diet, 24/7 duty call, and harsh living environments—to name a few—that affect their ability to rest and recover. This is quite different from athletes and other civilians, who, after a concussion, often are able to rest, sleep in a comfortable environment, and have ready access to medical care.

Signs of Mild TBI

To help you recognize more clearly signs and symptoms of mild TBI, let's separate them into four categories: physical, cognitive, behavioral, and emotional (VA/DoD 2009). Note that the examples given for each category below are not exhaustive. Also, some of these symptoms are short-term. For example, while it's not unusual for a service member to have headaches and cognitive problems one month after the injury, if he is still vomiting at that point, there may be a different medical problem that needs to be addressed. In the categories below, an asterisk next to a symptom indicates that it's typically acute (i.e., it would occur immediately after the event and subside more quickly), whereas those symptoms without an asterisk may last somewhat longer.

- **Physical problems:** headaches; sensitivity to light and noise; dizziness*; balance problems; tiring easily; sleep problems; pain; vomiting*; nausea*
- **Cognitive ("thinking") problems:** difficulty with attention, concentration, remembering; feeling confused*, disoriented*, foggy/zoned out*; being easily distracted; poor insight into one's problems; slow processing of information; slurred/incoherent speech*
- **Behavioral problems:** impulsiveness; aggressiveness; agitation; insensitivity toward others; disinhibition; childlike/childish behavior; poor self-control/judgment; passivity; dependence; lack of motivation; lack of spontaneity
- **Emotional ("feeling") problems:** irritability; anxiety; depression; apathy; emotional instability; poor self-image; personality change

What you probably noticed after reviewing these four categories is that there certainly are a lot of signs and symptoms associated with TBI. Also, several are probably familiar to you because they are symptoms of other medical and mental health conditions; for example, irritability, difficulty with concentration, sleep problems, and anxiety could all reflect post-traumatic stress. Because so many TBI symptoms are common in other conditions, it can be difficult to know whether what you're seeing is due to a TBI. In fact, concussive symptoms are extremely nonspecific and actually relatively common in the general population.

How Do You Know It's TBI?

Given the nonspecific nature of TBI symptoms and their overlap with other conditions, as well as the common experiencing of such symptoms in the general population, how can you really know whether your service member had a TBI? Fortunately, the Department of Defense (DoD) has instituted systematic screenings for TBIs in operational settings and at different points after deployment to help identify TBIs in service members closer to the time of injury (VA/DoD 2009). Diagnosing a TBI in theater is a two-step process. After any event that could have potentially caused a TBI, a service member has a brief screening. If that screening is positive, the person is then referred for a more comprehensive evaluation. Therefore, your daughter, for example, may already know she had a TBI because she was diagnosed with one when she was in theater. Both immediately after deployment and approximately three to six months later, service members also have to complete post-deployment questionnaires, parts of which screen for TBI. If someone screens positive on a post-deployment questionnaire, he or she is thoroughly evaluated and a determination is made about whether he or she had a TBI. Unfortunately, service members may underreport or deny symptoms on questionnaires and to health care providers because they believe admitting to symptoms may delay their ability to return to duty or because they do not want to admit to what they see as a weakness. So a screen may fail to capture what they are experiencing and they may never be referred for a comprehensive evaluation. And even if your service member is aware or learns that he or she sustained a TBI, he or she may not tell you.

We do know that those symptoms that best distinguish TBI from other problems, such as post-traumatic stress, are the physical ones—namely headaches, dizziness, balance problems, and sensitivity to light. In fact, headaches are the single most common complaint following mild TBI (VA/DoD 2009). However, because many of the problems listed earlier may actually stem from multiple sources (e.g., TBI, post-traumatic stress, pain, substance abuse, depression, sleep apnea), encourage your service member to set an appointment with a neuropsychologist or TBI or Neurocognitive Rehabilitation Clinic for a thorough evaluation. It's important to note that there is no perfect screen or test to diagnose a mild TBI. Although neuropsychologists administer tests to evaluate cognitive problems (e.g., poor memory, poor concentration), they actually rely on interview and a medical records review to diagnose a TBI. Neuropsychological testing is only used to assess cognitive complaints, and these tests can't determine the cause of symptoms (i.e., whether a TBI occurred or not). In some cases, your service member may have to first go to a primary care doctor or health care provider to get a referral to a neuropsychologist.

Recovery from Mild TBI

Most people who have sustained a mild TBI recover within hours or days, at most one to three months—very few have symptoms that persist beyond six months to a year (VA/DoD 2009). However, this assumes the individual has had or will have time to rest and recover from the injury. If your service member got rest and sleep after a TBI, recovery will be faster. If he or she continued to encounter demands and stress that impeded sleep and recuperation time, recovery will take longer. Yet full recovery is still expected.

The course of recovery also depends on the specific injury; whether other physical injuries or mental health conditions like post-traumatic stress or substance abuse are present; how the person perceives the injury and its effects; whether the person has had other head trauma; when he or she acknowledges and gets help for the TBI; and other factors (Alexander 1995; Essential Learning 2010; Kushner 1998). Because service members with combat-related TBI commonly minimize or delay reporting their problems, their recovery may be negatively affected or take longer. Additionally, longer recovery times and incomplete recoveries may occur after a service member has sustained multiple TBIs. However, if he or she has other issues such as mental health problems, sleep apnea, or alcohol or substance abuse problems (including abuse of prescription medications), these issues should be addressed first, in order to determine whether the symptoms are actually associated with those problems, rather than mild TBI.

In a minority of instances, service members who have sustained a mild TBI continue to have a constellation of problems a year or longer after the original injury (VA/DoD 2009). Post-concussive syndrome (PCS) may be indicated in these circumstances if no other issues (e.g., post-traumatic stress, depression, substance abuse) are present. Yet, until these other factors are examined, a neuropsychologist will not necessarily give a service member the diagnosis of PCS. The only way to truly determine whether lasting symptoms are due to a concussion is to treat all the other overlapping conditions. This is particularly important because misattributing symptoms to a TBI may lead providers to miss or mistreat other conditions.

How to Help

Arm yourself with the suggestions below so you're ready to assist your service member if he or she has had a mild TBI. Many of these recommendations are derived from the VA/DoD *Clinical Practice Guideline for Management of Concussion/mTBI* (2009) and the online course *The Fundamentals of Traumatic Brain Injury (TBI)* (Center for Deployment Psychology 2010).

Get informed, and stay positive. Education about mild TBI and its hopeful prognosis is very important for everyone involved. You and your service member should learn all you can about mild TBI. Use the resources listed in the back of this book (the Defense and Veterans Brain Injury Center website at www.dvbic.org is a good place to start), speak to TBI specialists, and if you do an Internet search, be sure to visit only accredited sites because a lot of misinformation has been posted about TBI.

Set the expectation that your service member will recover and will be able to return to duty, work, and/or do all the things he or she used to enjoy. This is particularly important, even if military duties did not allow adequate time for rest and recovery immediately following the injury and/or other medical or mental health problems complicate the recovery process. Normalize the physical, cognitive, behavioral, and emotional reactions your service member may be experiencing. This can help reduce everyone's anxiety and fears. Whether you use the word "concussion" or "mild TBI" in your conversation, convey a message of hope and recovery.

Remember that TBI is an event. Consider a TBI as you would a broken arm, not a disease. If you broke your arm, you would probably experience pain, throbbing, and numbness, but eventually you would recover. If asked about it, you might say something like "I broke my arm and am still having some pain and trouble from it, but it's getting better." Similarly, we encourage individuals who have sustained a TBI to regard it like any other physical injury from which recovery is expected. Although there may be lifelong effects, especially after a severe injury, and research on the effects of multiple TBIs is ongoing, TBIs—especially mild TBIs and blast-related TBIs—do not usually worsen over time (i.e., there are no degenerative effects). Currently, researchers don't know whether mild TBI resulting from blasts is different from other concussions, but some of the research suggests they may not be that different.

Ensure that your service member gets a full physical workup. Encourage your service member to have a thorough physical workup with a primary care doctor or other health care provider including lab work to rule out contributing issues. Since symptoms of sleep apnea overlap with those of mild TBI, encourage your service member to report problems like fatigue, snoring, concentration problems, and headaches to the provider, who may refer him or her for a full sleep workup. Also recommend that your service member speak to his or her provider or medical team about the appropriateness of using certain medications because some may have sedating effects, which can exacerbate problems with attention and fatigue.

Help your service member tackle specific symptoms. Because another important part of recovery is sufficient rest and treatment of specific symptoms, such as sleep, headaches, pain, anxiety, anger, or depression, encourage your service member to work with a health care provider, mental health professional, and/or multidisciplinary team to gradually increase his or her physical activities and to target those symptoms and complaints that are most distressing to him or her. For example, if your daughter is experiencing headaches, recommend that she work with a health care provider who knows how to manage headaches, and consider using some of the pain management techniques we outlined earlier in this chapter if they apply. If your daughter has migraines, medication may be warranted, as well as a consultation with a neurologist.

Since sleep problems can worsen pain and vice versa, if sleep problems are part of the picture for your service member it's crucial that he or she address them head-on. Poor sleep in particular can really do a number on emotional and physical well-being and delay recovery from TBI. Therefore, emphasize the importance of getting help to improve both the quality and quantity of your service member's sleep. You may find the sleep tips and strategies in chapter 7 to be useful for the entire family.

Talk to your service member about avoiding risky activities. Remind your service member to use healthy behaviors and to refrain from high-risk activities while recuperating, in order to prevent being injured again. Having a second injury can lead to longer recovery times and the possibility of ongoing symptoms or a less than full recovery. This means avoiding alcohol and other substances, caffeine, and energy drinks; not taking pseudoephedrine unless recommended or prescribed by a health care provider, and not participating in risky sports or activities. It also means wearing protective gear like seat belts and helmets.

Discuss ways to offset challenges. Brainstorm with your service member simple yet resourceful strategies to compensate for difficulties remembering or concentrating. For example, you can encourage your son to develop and stick to a daily routine; regularly carry a schedule or day planner to remind himself of appointments and meetings; jot down notes throughout the day to serve as reminders later; and focus on one task at a time. If your service member already carries a smart phone or tablet, using relevant apps to reinforce these coping skills can be a winning combination. Your service member could also receive training in the use of these devices through assistive technology services or occupational therapy. If your service member is attending school, she will be eligible for specialized services. For more information, see chapter 2, "Services for Disabled Students."

Encourage your service member to share with others. Talk to your service member about how to tell other important people in his or her life that he or she is recuperating from a mild TBI or has a history of concussions. This will allow those people to better support your service member. It's key that your service member not feel embarrassed or ashamed if, for example, she needs to ask for more time to complete tasks. Remember that sharing this information with others should be your service member's decision, however, not yours.

If your service member's symptoms persist despite his or her working with a multidisciplinary team and trying different strategies, encourage him or her to talk to those health care providers about what might account for the continuing symptoms and the lack of improvement. There could be a host of factors undermining your service member's mental and physical health, such as post-traumatic stress, anxiety, alcohol or substance abuse, sleep deprivation, depression, pain, sleep apnea, and medication issues, as well as family or relationship problems or motivational or compensation issues. Once such problems are identified, they should be targeted in your service member's treatment plan.

Moderate or Severe TBI

If your service member experienced a moderate to severe TBI, an excellent resource is the comprehensive family caregiver guide called *Traumatic Brain Injury: A Guide for Caregivers of Service Members and Veterans* found at www.traumaticbraininjury atoz.org/Caregivers-Journey/Caregiver-Guides.aspx. It focuses on how to care not only for your service member, but also for yourself.

Tinnitus

Roscoe can remember the loud boom from a mortar round that landed near him early one morning in Afghanistan. He was thrown back, blacked out for some time, and learned later that he'd sustained a TBI. He had experienced many close calls with explosions like this one during his three previous deployments. Since returning from this last deployment, however, he has been plagued by not only persistent back pain, but also a constant ringing in both ears. No matter what he tries, it just won't go away.

Tinnitus affects millions of people at varying levels, including service members. Commonly described as "ringing" in the ear, tinnitus is the top VA service-connected disability for veterans who have returned from Iraq and Afghanistan (ATA 2012d). Tinnitus involves "hearing" sounds in one or both ears when there actually is no external sound—while the person with tinnitus can hear the sound, nobody else can. This "ringing" may come and go, or it may be present constantly, and it can range from soft to loud. Although "ringing" is the most commonly reported sound, some individuals hear sounds like buzzing, hissing, clicking, screeching, or whistling (ATA 2012a; Mayes 2010). As you can imagine, this can be highly annoying and distracting, disrupting a person's ability to concentrate, work, socialize, and sleep, to say the least. For some military personnel, tinnitus may also cue unwanted memories associated with wartime experiences (Giles 2012).

What Triggers the Ringing?

Although the exact physiological cause of tinnitus is not known, the most common trigger is loud noise. Loss of hearing or head or neck injuries may also activate or worsen tinnitus. Tinnitus can also be a symptom of various medical conditions (e.g., cardiovascular disease, hypothyroidism or hyperthyroidism, diabetes, fibromyalgia, tumors, jaw misalignment) or ear problems (e.g., infections, earwax buildup, dislocated ear bones), or it can be related to food allergies or medication side effects (ATA 2012a; Mayes 2010). Because of service members' frequent exposure to loud noise—for example, during combat and training activities and from loud aircraft—they can be at risk for tinnitus (Giles 2012). For those who have served in Iraq or Afghanistan, where exposure to loud noises from different types of blasts has been relatively common, as in Roscoe's story, this risk may be even higher. According to clinical audiologist J. L. Mayes (2010), there is a higher rate of prolonged tinnitus in service members with war experience (50%) than in the general US population (10% to 15%), as well as in individuals with chronic pain or migraines. In addition, veterans with underlying mood disorders and insomnia may experience tinnitus as more disabling (Baum n.d.).

How Can You Help?

If your service member is complaining of ringing in his or her ears and has never received help, one of the best things you can do is assist him or her in securing a medical appointment with an audiologist or an ear, nose, and throat (ENT) doctor who has experience diagnosing and treating tinnitus and can determine whether there is a medical cause. If it's determined that the tinnitus is the result of a health or dental problem, a health care or dental provider can treat the condition and help relieve the tinnitus (Mayes 2010). In many cases, however, there is no medical root; if this is the situation for your service member, encourage him or her to have an open discussion with a health care provider who is knowledgeable about tinnitus and available treatment options, some of which we summarize below. While many of these approaches can provide varying degrees of relief, there is no cure for tinnitus (ATA 2012b; Mayes 2010). Keep in mind that the following is not an exhaustive list of tinnitus treatments, and often multiple strategies will be combined and tailored to meet your service member's unique needs.

Nonmedical Treatment Approaches for Tinnitus

Counseling/therapy. Working with a therapist, individuals diagnosed with tinnitus can learn strategies to cope with the emotional components of tinnitus—that is, how to reduce their negative reactions and responses to it. *Cognitive behavioral therapy* (CBT) is a type of therapy that can help an individual with tinnitus identify how negative thoughts and beliefs about tinnitus (e.g., *I can't live with this awful ringing in my ears*) are influencing his or her emotions (e.g., feeling defeated) and behaviors (e.g., withdrawing from activities and people). In CBT, the therapist helps the individual to challenge and change these types of unhelpful thoughts, which in turn helps to decrease negative emotions and unhealthy behaviors (ATA 2012e; Mayes 2010).

Mind-body techniques. Meditation, deep breathing, imagery, distraction, biofeedback (the ability to control body activities that typically occur outside of conscious control, such as breathing), yoga, and staying mentally active (e.g., engaging in interests, socializing) can help individuals focus their attention away from their tinnitus. These strategies may be woven into CBT or other therapies, but they can also be learned on their own. Many of these strategies have a calming effect because they help reduce emotional and physiological stress, thereby helping the individual to cope with tinnitus. These approaches are some of the same mind-body techniques used to address pain, which we described earlier in this chapter (ATA 2012e; Mayes 2010).

Sound therapy. The purpose of sound therapy for tinnitus is to make it easier for individuals to ignore their tinnitus by increasing the presence of outside sounds. This helps make the tinnitus less obvious. There are three general strategies: (1) using sound to soothe or relax the listener; (2) providing a background sound that the tinnitus can blend into; and (3) using sound to actively draw the listener's attention away from his or her tinnitus. Different types of sound devices can be used, including tabletop sound machines, on-ear/wearable sound generators, or music devices (e.g., MP3 players). The volume of the sounds used depends on the specific type of sound therapy. In formal sound therapy for tinnitus, a tinnitus specialist or audiologist provides guidance regarding volume levels and/or sets the volume depending on the type of sound device being used (ATA 2012e; Mayes 2010). Below are examples of sound therapy:

- *Tinnitus masking therapy.* In this type of sound therapy, white noise (a neutral background sound) is used to partially or completely muffle or "mask" tinnitus. While many individuals gain some relief from this approach, some do not because their tinnitus is too loud or they find the loudness required of the external noise for "masking" the tinnitus too disruptive (Mayes 2010).

- *Tinnitus retraining therapy (TRT).* TRT uses a combination of education, counseling, and sound therapy to help individuals get used to their tinnitus. The goal is to no longer be aware of or be bothered by the tinnitus. Individuals work with a formally trained TRT specialist to follow a strict schedule of certain amounts of sound therapy for several months to a year (Mayes 2010).

- *Progressive tinnitus management (PTM).* The aim of PTM is to give the individual the responsibility of day-to-day management of his or her tinnitus. An interdisciplinary team including an audiologist, an ENT doctor, and a cognitive behavioral therapist helps educate the individual on tinnitus, develops a sound-based therapy that fits the individual's needs, and ensures the individual has proper referrals and access to clinical services as well as other resources to self-manage his or her tinnitus (Henry et al. 2009). PTM is offered at most VHA Medical Centers as well as the Walter Reed National Military Medical Center. Contact your service member's VHA Medical Center or military treatment facility to see whether this service is available.

Hearing loss strategies. About half of those with tinnitus also have hearing loss. Therefore, it's critical for individuals with tinnitus to have a hearing test to see whether they have hearing loss and to get hearing aids if needed. Some individuals with both tinnitus and hearing loss end up gaining partial or total relief from tinnitus while wearing their hearing aids because the devices make it easier for them to ignore their tinnitus in the presence of external sounds (ATA 2012e; Mayes 2010).

Healthy lifestyle. Those with tinnitus are encouraged to develop and stick to a healthy routine, including regular exercise as approved by a health care provider, a proper diet in which certain foods and drinks that might exacerbate tinnitus (e.g., caffeine, sugar, salt) are avoided, and good sleep practices. Sleep problems are common in those with tinnitus; therefore, it's important to develop healthy sleep habits (ATA 2012c; Mayes 2010). The healthy sleep strategies we describe in chapter 7 may help.

A Special Note about Medications

According to an article in *Military Medical & Veterans Affairs Forum*, "There are no specific tinnitus drugs available today, so doctors may prescribe off-label anti-depressants or pain-killers for troops suffering from tinnitus, which offers temporary relief in some cases, but may result in severe side effects or require repeated, painful injections" ("Troops with Tinnitus" 2012, 15).

You may hear about medications or supplements claiming to "cure" tinnitus—on television, on the Internet, or in print—and be tempted to encourage your service member to try them. However, there is no scientific research that indicates these medications or supplements are effective at all. So be careful not to be misled by such false claims. Alert your service member about this too!

Severe Medical Injuries

John, a twenty-two-year-old married soldier, sustained an IED blast early in his deployment that resulted in a moderate TBI, severe burns, shrapnel lodged in his back, and the loss of a leg. His twenty-one-year-old wife, whom he'd married before he left, met him at the military treatment facility (MTF) where he was being treated in the casualty care unit. The couple didn't have much support because John was estranged from his family, and while he enjoyed a close relationship with *her* parents, they lived hundreds of miles away and couldn't come to the MTF.

After several surgeries, he lost significant weight, felt down and hopeless, and became extremely anxious whenever his wife left his bedside. He was convinced that his life and future were at a dead end—he was getting out of the military, but what work could he do? Although John had strong interests in mechanics and carpentry, he was sure he could never do that type of work with his injuries. He just prayed his wife wouldn't leave him. She and her parents were all he had.

Severe medical injuries sustained by those deployed to Iraq and Afghanistan like John include those from bullets, motor vehicle accidents, falls, and blasts, and not infrequently multiple mechanisms of injury all at once. Of these, blasts from improvised explosive devices (IEDs), mortar rounds, rocket-propelled grenades, roadside bombs, and other explosives have been a major source of life-threatening wounds including TBI and serious limb and organ damage (DVBIC 2012a).

In spite of today's modern weaponry, more service members from the conflicts in Iraq and Afghanistan as compared to previous wars have survived such threats, because of better body and head protection, as well as improved battlefield medicine and technology. These innovations include enhanced rapid transport of seriously injured service members from a war zone to military treatment facilities and longer-term rehabilitation hospitals and transitional programs.

Although today's lifesaving medical advancements have been nothing short of miraculous, we still have much to learn about the impact of blasts on the human mind and body. Seriously wounded service members such as John who survive these blasts have recently been identified as having *polytrauma injuries*, which the VHA has defined as "concurrent injury to two or more body parts or systems that results in cognitive, physical, psychological or other psychosocial impairments" (Dobscha et al. 2008, 1). Such impairments include TBI, lost limbs, auditory or visual impairments, spinal cord injury, post-traumatic stress, and other mental health conditions.

Polytrauma injuries present challenges for service members and their loved ones, as well as the medical community, because the complex toll they inflict on the body and mind often requires incredible amounts of coordinated care. For instance, a service member like John may sustain an injury resulting not only from the pressure of a blast wave, but also from shrapnel, impact with a hard surface, and then inhalation of toxic fumes ignited by the blast. The cumulative effects of such injuries on the brain and body can require long periods of recovery and rehabilitation.

In order to address these serious and complex injuries, the VHA and DoD have established state-of-the-art acute and long-term care facilities starting with in-theater combat stress clinics and hospitals staffed with trauma surgeons and neurosurgeons. Following emergency care, service members seriously injured during overseas deployments are most often transported to Landstuhl Regional Medical Center in Germany and then to stateside casualty care units at military facilities. Because of the increased need for treatment of multiple complex injuries since the start of the War on Terror, the VHA has established a Polytrauma System of Care including five regionally based VHA Polytrauma Rehabilitation Centers, four Polytrauma Transitional Rehabilitation Programs, twenty-three Polytrauma Network Sites, eighty-seven Polytrauma Support Clinic Teams, and thirty-eight Polytrauma Points of Contact. To find your nearest VHA Polytrauma facility, visit www.polytrauma.va.gov/system-of-care.

A Service Member's Pain: A Wave of Responses

During deployment, Rafael was shot in the neck by a sniper and was medevaced for care stateside. He was the only one wounded in his squad during the ambush. He hasn't shared with anybody that he has been having crying spells whenever he thinks about his battle buddies and that he's planning to return to his combat position as soon as he can—otherwise he feels as if he's letting his buddies down "big time." To Rafael, they're his brothers—his family now—more than his mom, dad, and sisters. While his physical pain from the bullet wound is gradually subsiding, his guilt and self-blame about being the only one sent home are keeping him awake at night.

When a service member returns from deployment with a serious injury, he or she may end up transitioning back to full-duty status, moving to limited-duty status, or converting to veteran status. Service members' reactions to their injuries vary based on their background, their type of injuries, their circle of support, and many other variables. Still, there is a set of responses common to most seriously injured service members.

Denial

My son never called me when he got shot or hurt. Several months later he would bring it up, and just pushed through the pain and did his job. (Tiffany)

Perhaps without even knowing it, some wounded service members like Rafael use denial as a shield, to protect themselves from fully acknowledging that they have sustained a life-altering injury. Denial temporarily blocks distressing emotions such as feeling out of control, feeling helpless, or feeling damaged, as well as acceptance of the injury. And the military mind-set reinforces denial—those values of strength, courage, and self-sacrifice are inconsistent with admitting vulnerabilities including physical or psychological limitations. Also, active-duty service members who want to stay in the military may deny an injury or underreport their symptoms for fear that if they admit problems, their job or career will be jeopardized or they will be medically discharged or retired from the military.

Since denial will ultimately slow your service member's recovery, we encourage you to be on the lookout for it. Your service member may need help from an outside person such as clergy, a chaplain or spiritual advisor, or mental health provider to come to terms with what has happened. Joining other injured veterans in a support group may also be helpful, as may reading about injured veterans who have overcome great odds or listening to their testimonials on websites like Make the Connection (maketheconnection.net).

Loss after Loss

Although your injured service member will probably not talk to you directly about how he or she is feeling, it's common for those who have experienced a notable injury to feel sadness or grief over losing or damaging some part of their physical being and the life and abilities they enjoyed before. This is especially true for those service members who have disfiguring injuries (e.g., burns, facial wounds) or severe disabilities (e.g., amputations, blindness) and believe that these wounds have scarred their "warrior" strength and character. They may believe that others now perceive them as defective or damaged, weak, or unattractive and may start to internalize these negative characterizations. This can lead to self-loathing or self-disdain and result in withdrawal or detachment from friends and family. On top of this, injured service members may have lost one or more fellow service members at the time they were injured, so they may feel tremendous grief or guilt at having survived. In the story above, Rafael is experiencing a deep sense of loss over being separated from his comrades who are still deployed.

Pay special attention to whether your service member might be suffering in silence, burdened by loss and low self-worth, and again consider encouraging him or her to talk to a service member or veteran with similar experience or to clergy, a chaplain, or spiritual advisor, or mental health provider. The After Deployment website (afterdeployment.org/topics-physical-injury) offers information that can help you support your service member on the road to recovery from physical injury.

Shaken Identity

While Carina, a medic, was traveling in a convoy in Afghanistan, the vehicle in which she was riding with two other service members was hit by an IED blast. Her two companions died of their wounds. As for Carina, her multiple injuries included a serious spinal cord injury and necessitated reconstructive surgery to her right shoulder and elbow. Carina had loved her job, and she felt lost about her career when she realized she couldn't remain a medic. She also couldn't stop thinking about the two who had died and how much anguish their spouses and kids, about whom she'd heard a lot, must be going through. She wished it could have been her instead of them.

As you might expect, the strong military identity that many service members adopt can be badly shaken by a physical injury, as we see in the case of Carina. This identity struggle can be as painful as the injury itself, as service members come to terms with a world in which they no longer are able to perform the same duties (e.g., Carina can't serve in the medical field anymore—she can only hold a desk job) or even remain in their chosen career: the military. For somebody like Carina, aspirations of moving up the ranks and proudly serving until retirement age may be shattered as the reality of the devastating effects of the physical injury sinks in.

Be aware of the identity issues your service member may be wrestling with in addition to physical problems, because these can take a significant toll. You can help by pointing out and positively reinforcing the many roles your service member inhabits besides his or her military one. For example, invite your daughter who is also a mother, sister, pianist, friend, mentor, and church volunteer to see her multiple strengths—her life need not be defined by her military identity alone.

Physical and Mental Health Go Hand in Hand

When so many threads of a service member's life unravel at once as a result of a life-threatening event, it's not uncommon for mental health conditions like depression, anxiety, or substance abuse to co-occur with TBI and other more severe physical injuries. In fact, in a study of combat soldiers, researchers found that mild TBI involving loss of consciousness was strongly associated with both post-traumatic stress and depression (Hoge et al. 2008). We know that in the case of polytrauma, the traumatic events surrounding service members' physical injuries can be extremely disturbing to their psyche and thus set the stage for conditions like acute or chronic post-traumatic stress.

In addition, for some service members with physical injuries, the feelings of loss, grief, and sadness we described earlier come to interfere with their ability to function on a daily basis or move forward in life. For example, your son may be enveloped by a clinical depression as described in chapter 3 and need professional help.

It's also quite normal for injured service members to experience waves of anxiety about their future. So many questions arise: "Can I stay in the military? If I can't, how am I going to support my family?" "How will this affect the health benefits for my wife and children?" "What will my buddies think of me if I take off the uniform?" If this "what if" thinking and other signs of worry and anxiety become pervasive and debilitating, your service member may now be faced with a level of anxiety that warrants outside help. Please refer to chapter 3 for more information about this type of anxiety.

Thus, if your service member has experienced a serious physical injury, it's quite likely he or she is also struggling with mental health issues that can exacerbate the physical pain, in turn worsening his or her emotional distress and impeding recovery. Bottom line: your service member may need your assistance with not only physical wounds, but also emotional injuries.

Triggers

Be aware that when service members' pain from a physical injury is set off by something as simple as cold weather, rain, or a bad night's sleep, it can take their mind right back to the traumatic event that led to their physical injury or its aftermath. Suddenly they may find themselves feeling as if they're back at the time and place of the injury. If your service member is triggered like this, he or she may feel out of control or disoriented, become flooded with powerful images of the event, or even have flashbacks. If this happens, let your service member know that this is not unusual, and explain what may be going on so it seems less scary or crazy. Also, help your service member develop ways to stabilize or "ground" himself or herself should such memories be triggered again. Share the following "grounding" tips, and have your service member pick one or two to practice:

- Focus your attention on your immediate surroundings and silently name the things you see in the room or around you one by one.

- Position your feet firmly on the floor or carpet and hold tightly to the arms of a chair or couch, focusing on what your feet and hands feel like and the sense of being tethered.
- Repeat silently to yourself a message that conveys safety and a sense of the present, such as *I'm safe; I'm back in the states. I'm not deployed. I'm okay* or *My name is Kelly. I'm twenty-five years old. Today is September 1, 2013.*

A Parent's Pain: Coping with the Aftermath

> *I have an amazing husband and three other wonderful children who all love my son as much as I do. We're a family. What doesn't kill us makes us stronger. WE ARE STRONG!* (Anchal)

If your service member has sustained a life-altering injury, coping with the aftermath can be extremely challenging and test your resiliency like never before. It can alter the way you view many things, including your role as a parent, your future, your service member's future, and the military. There's no doubt that caring for someone with polytrauma injuries can change the focus of your life and be overwhelming.

At the same time, we have been inspired by the stories we hear from parents of severely injured service members—mothers who have forged closer relationships with their injured son and other family members; fathers who have turned this extremely challenging experience into a powerful, positive journey of growth culminating in their giving back to other military families in need of support; and parents who have gained insights into themselves and their place in the world that have brought them new meaning and purpose.

A Mix of Reactions

While each parent may ultimately reach a place of insight and connection, they generally must navigate through many emotional responses as they come to grips with the reality of their service member's injury. Initially, it's quite normal to feel shock, fear, and even horror. Even though you may have told yourself that such an injury could happen to your service member and mentally prepared for it, that it has actually happened can be an incredible shock to your system. You may be in complete disbelief and feel sick, anxious, or unable to sleep or concentrate on anything other than your service member's well-being.

In addition to experiencing shock, you may engage in denial or wishful thinking—going back and forth between denying or minimizing that your service member has been seriously wounded and beginning to accept that it has occurred. You might find yourself thinking, *This is all a dream. It hasn't really happened*; *It couldn't be* my *son who's been harmed*; or *The injuries aren't as bad as the doctors are saying. My daughter will be fine soon.*

Besides denial or wishful thinking, it's also normal to feel really angry that your service member has been harmed. You may even feel resentment, thinking to yourself: *After all that she has sacrificed for the military, why couldn't they protect her? Why her and not somebody else?* It can seem downright unfair, and you may find yourself upset with the military or a higher power that this is happening to your family, or you may feel angry or unforgiving toward the "enemy" in the area of operations where your service member was injured.

Your anger may be joined by sheer grief and sadness as you recognize the long-term effects of the injury on not only your service member (and his or her partner or children, if applicable), but also your whole family. You may be overcome by feelings of loss and even nostalgia as you realize how many things will change because of this life-altering event. For example, you may feel deep loss as you see how helpless and vulnerable your injured son is—how dependent he is on you and his treatment providers—in stark contrast with how strong, independent, and full of life he was before he deployed.

If you encouraged your son or daughter to join the military—for example, to do something meaningful for our country or to follow in the footsteps of family members who served—you also may now feel the weight of guilt. In these instances, you may repeatedly tell yourself something like *If only I hadn't encouraged her to go into the military, she wouldn't be suffering.* In addition, if you are or were in the military yourself, your son or daughter's injury may be emotionally and physically upsetting or triggering, causing you panic, agitation, or nightmares. It may take you back to your own military service and traumatic experiences when you were in harm's way. If so, please review the "grounding" strategies described earlier.

If you are caring for an injured service member, let us reassure you that each of these reactions and thoughts is normal. However, in your effort to support and care for your son or daughter, it's easy to neglect your own needs, extending yourself up to and at times beyond your breaking point. Because maintaining your own health and well-being is essential to your ability to provide support to others, we recommend that you read chapter 7, in which we review a wide range of strategies for caring for yourself while caring for your service member.

Conclusion

Deployments have resulted in physical problems for many of our nation's troops including mild TBI, back and knee injuries, and tinnitus, as well as severe polytrauma injuries for a small but signigicant number of military personnel that require lengthy hospitalizations and rehabilitation. Fortunately, advances in military medicine are saving more lives on the battlefield and leading to faster identification of both life-threatening and non-life-threatening physical injuries. The information in this chapter will hopefully help you more clearly recognize the signs and symptoms of physical injuries in your service member, including pain, which can take on a debilitating life of its own and worsen both physical and mental health problems. If you are presently caring for your service member who was injured while serving our country, remember that you are not alone in your struggles and it's to be expected that you will experience a variety of emotions. At the same time, we hope this chapter has given you ideas for bolstering your service member's physical and emotional strength.

Chapter Tips

- Be on the lookout for signs and symptoms of "wear and tear" injuries from deployment.
- Remember that your service member is likely to downplay injuries like TBI and will need your encouragement to acknowledge them.
- Validate the pain your service member is experiencing without pitying him or her. The last thing your military son or daughter wants is pity.
- Help your service member learn as much as possible about physical injuries and pain, as well as co-occurring mental health problems. Information is power.
- Urge your son or daughter to channel that military "can-do attitude" into overcoming stigma about physical complaints and getting appropriate help.
- Set a tone of hope and positive recovery. Promote this attitude among family members and others in your service member's life.
- Focus on what your service member *can* do, not on what he or she *can't* do, even with physical limitations or pain.
- Encourage your service member to learn about the success stories of other service members recovering from physical injuries and to participate in organizations and activities that promote healing.
- For some suggested sources of further information and support, turn to the list of resources at the back of the book.

chapter 5

How to Get Your Veteran the Health Care He or She Deserves

It is wise for parents to research veteran benefits and care for returning military health problems. Find out who to ask for veteran needs. (Gerard)

One of the greatest advantages that military service provides is access to health care. If your service member is staying in the military, you are probably aware of this valuable benefit. However, when your service member leaves the military, he or she will most probably be eligible for a variety of health care services. Even if your son or daughter is currently physically and mentally healthy, the health care available to veterans may be useful to him or her at some point. The purpose of this chapter is to outline the major health care benefits and services for veterans (i.e., those who have separated from service or medically retired) and certain members of the Reserves and National Guard. We'll describe the process of enrolling in health care through the Veterans Health Administration (VHA), as well as non-VHA services, with an emphasis on assisting your veteran in securing quality mental health care.

Note that there are many rules regarding eligibility for VHA health care—not all veterans, members of the National Guard, and members of the Reserves qualify. We will not be able to cover all these circumstances. If your service member does not currently qualify, he or she may qualify later, because eligibility for care often changes, as do service members' circumstances. You should encourage your service member to meet with a VHA representative from the Business/Member Services Department to determine whether he or she is eligible for care. Also inquire through your service member's particular branch of service. Because there are many types of military discharge including honorable, general discharge, discharge under other than honorable conditions, bad conduct discharge, and dishonorable discharge, if you're not sure whether your service member qualifies, have him or her apply anyway. Go to this US Department of Veterans Affairs (VA) website for more information: www.va.gov/healthbenefits/apply/returning_servicemembers.asp. If your service member is turned down, encourage him or her to meet with a Veterans Service Officer or a member of a veterans advocacy group to find out whether he or she can appeal this decision. For information on health care options for active-duty service members or for members of the Reserves and National Guard who don't have access to health care through the VHA, please see the headings "For Families" and "Health Care" in the list of resources at the end of this book, which will help you find information on options such as TRICARE and Military OneSource.

VA Health Care and Benefits

There are a number of federal agencies, most notably those within the VA, specifically designed to assist veterans. While the general public refers to both the Veterans Benefits Administration (VBA) and the Veterans Health Administration (VHA) as simply the VA, these are in fact separate divisions. Among other services, the VBA administers educational benefits and vocational rehabilitation and determines whether veterans' injuries are related to military service and thus qualify for compensation. Other functions of the VBA include administrating home loans and life insurance. For additional information about the VBA, go to www.vba.va.gov/VBA.

The VHA, on the other hand, provides medical care to veterans, operating 152 medical centers and over fourteen hundred

Community-Based Outpatient Clinics (CBOCs). Under certain circumstances, the VHA also provides services for family members of veterans. For example, a new program currently provides financial and health care support to caregivers of Operation Iraqi Freedom (OIF), Operation Enduring Freedom (OEF), or Operation New Dawn (OND) veterans with significant emotional or physical disabilities. Turn to chapter 7 to learn more about the Caregiver Support Program.

VHA Health Care Benefits

> *She is under VA medical care. Since we do not live near her, she has scheduled appointments etc. on her own. We have offered to help.*
> (Shannon)

Currently, a service member who served two years' active duty or was deployed to a combat zone and received either an honorable discharge or a discharge under honorable conditions is eligible for health care. Other benefits include a one-time dental exam within 180 days from the date of discharge (if there was no dental exam within the last six months of service). Those who were deployed as part of OEF/OIF/OND may be eligible for health care through the VHA for the first five years after discharge for any care considered "combat-related."

Eligibility for noncombat veterans and for OEF/OIF/OND veterans after the initial five years depends on a number of factors, including income and whether they have a service-connected disability or are claiming other service-related issues. A portion of the "Application for Health Benefits" (1010EZ form) includes a financial assessment or means test, which determines whether a veteran's income exceeds the financial eligibility threshold (although certain conditions may exempt a veteran from this threshold). Once enrolled, veterans without a service-connected disability are usually required to complete a Health Benefits Renewal or 1010EZR form every year, which also includes a means test to determine whether or not co-pays will be required.

While the process of determining whether your son or daughter qualifies for health care may be challenging, actual enrollment in the VHA is easy and can be done online or in person, typically through VHA's Business/Member Services. All your service member needs to enroll is identification, a copy of his or her DD214, and a completed 1010EZ form.

Once your service member enrolls, we strongly suggest you encourage an appointment with a primary care provider for a checkup. If the enrollment or appointment process is at all confusing or overwhelming, know that all major VHA Medical Centers employ Operation Enduring Freedom (OEF), Operation Iraqi Freedom (OIF), and Operantion New Dawn (OND) Program Managers or Case Managers (typically social workers) to help recently separated combat veterans who served in either Afghanistan or Iraq (or both) enroll and negotiate the early phases of getting care. The goal of this program is to make receiving care seamless, allowing service members to obtain care with limited hassle.

Veterans who suffer from physical or psychological injuries that occurred during their service may qualify for additional VHA services and even disability compensation. While your service member can apply for service-connected disability on his or her own, it's best to find someone from the VBA or a service organization like the Disabled American Veterans (DAV), the Order of the Purple Heart, American Vets (AMVETS), or a county veteran service organization to help. The VA has a web page of benefits fact sheets including a section on disabilities at www.vba.va.gov/vba/benefits/factsheets.asp.

Calling All Young, Healthy Veterans!

Have your soldier register and apply for veteran benefits. (Bridget)

Younger veterans are not always quick to enroll in health care, nor do they necessarily know what benefits they are eligible for. Although the Department of Defense (DoD) typically briefs those separating from service about health benefits, at this early stage of reintegration your service member may be focused on spending time with family and/or friends or may see himself or herself as young and healthy and therefore not in need of health care. A common misconception is that veterans are eligible for VHA health care only if they have a recognized disability as a result of their service. Consequently, your veteran may be surprised that he or she is eligible for health care benefits. Some people also misperceive the VHA as primarily serving an older generation of veterans, not knowing that it has changed significantly and now offers relevant services for newly discharged service members. Even if your service member is "fine," it's good to have him or her discuss any minor medical concerns with a VHA health care provider because if some medical or mental health issue begins to develop into a more significant problem, it's important for this information to be well documented in VHA records. Additionally, if your service member is filing a claim for one or more conditions related to his or her service (service-connected disability), it can be helpful to have these conditions documented in his or her VHA medical record.

If You've Seen One VHA Medical Center, You've Seen One VHA Medical Center

While there are plenty of standard protocols within the larger VHA system that all clinicians follow, each VHA Medical Center has its own distinct culture. The layouts of VHA Medical Centers vary considerably, and veterans' accessibility to them also varies. Consequently, one VHA may "feel" more friendly and accessible than another. Some VHA hospitals are closely associated with a university, allowing for the training of new doctors, mental health professionals (also known as behavioral health professionals), nurses, and other allied health professionals. The environment and culture of a training institution certainly can affect veterans' experience of treatment and care. For example, your son may receive medical or mental health care from a trainee under the supervision of a licensed professional, which has both advantages and disadvantages. On the positive side, he gets to see a younger clinician with whom it may be easier to relate and who is being trained and supervised in state-of-the-art interventions. The trade-off is that trainees come and go. While it can be upsetting to your veteran when a trainee leaves at the end of his or her term, the good news is that VHA medical documentation is excellent, making it easy for a new clinician to quickly catch up on your veteran's history and treatment by reviewing his or her chart.

To summarize, it's not only important for service members to enroll in the VHA as soon as they are eligible, but also good for them to physically go to their local VHA to familiarize themselves with the facility. It also may make sense for your veteran to meet with members of the VHA staff prior to scheduling an initial checkup, to help determine whether it feels like a place where he or she will be comfortable receiving care.

VHA Mental Health Care

In order to obtain mental health services at a VHA Medical Center, veterans typically need to request care through their primary care provider or by directly contacting the mental health service. Usually the first mental health visit your veteran will have is a triage appointment, in which a clinician conducts a brief screen of mental health problems and then refers your veteran to an intake appointment. The intake appointment is a detailed interview to both ascertain your veteran's mental health concerns and obtain relevant personal history. A treatment plan is then developed in collaboration with your veteran. VHA mental health care is predominantly delivered by social workers, psychologists, nurses, psychiatrists, and their respective trainees. The VHA actively trains clinicians in evidence-based treatments, which means that the interventions provided have been studied and are considered effective.

VHA Community-Based Outpatient Clinics (CBOCs)

CBOCs are VHA medical clinics located in mostly rural areas, with the purpose of providing medical and mental health services to veterans and their families in these communities. Veterans in rural areas may receive primary care and mental health services at a CBOC and visit one of the larger VHA Medical Centers, located generally in urban centers, only for more complex services and procedures. CBOCs are generally extremely busy, however, and may have lengthy wait times. CBOCs typically work closely with their nearest VHA Medical Center in order to provide state-of-the-art treatment; for example, at these clinics patients may be able, through telemedicine services, to receive care from an expert clinician located hundreds of miles away at a VHA Medical Center.

Vet Centers (Readjustment Counseling Services)

Opened as storefront counseling centers embedded in communities following the Vietnam War, Vet Centers are another part of the federal VHA system. Many Vet Centers are staffed by licensed mental health professionals who are also veterans. Some veterans find it helpful to speak with such a counselor, who hasn't just read about military service but lived it. A goal of Vet Centers is to provide a hassle-free experience as much as possible in comparison to VHA Medical Centers, making it easier for veterans to receive services. For example, while typically a veteran can see a mental health professional at a VHA Medical Center only by appointment except in cases of psychiatric emergency, Vet Centers often accommodate "walk-ins." There are approximately three hundred Vet Centers across the country, most of them in areas with large veteran populations. The primary service offered is counseling, with a specialized focus on providing mental health care to war-zone veterans, military sexual assault survivors, and bereaved family members (of recently deceased active-duty service members), as well as couples and families in need of counseling. Some Vet Centers work closely with VHA Medical Centers so they have access to a part-time VHA psychiatrist, for example, to assist with issues such as medication management. Many Vet Centers don't assist service members in applying for service-connected VA benefits but can refer them to organizations that do.

Similar to VHA Medical Centers, each Vet Center has its own culture. There is an important difference, however, between Vet Centers and VHA Medical Centers (including CBOCs) regarding confidentiality of records. While records may be shared between the DoD and VHA Medical Center personnel, Vet Center records are not accessible by either of the other systems without the written permission of the client. However, Vet Center clinicians have the ability to review their clients' records in the DoD and VHA medical systems. Make sure your service member knows about this added level of confidentiality inherent in Vet Centers, which may make him or her feel more comfortable seeking help there versus at a VHA Medical Center or CBOC. In addition, Vet Centers typically are more flexible than VHA Medical Centers or CBOCs in also providing mental health care to the spouse and/or family members of any veteran receiving counseling there. If you're interested in locating a VHA Medical Center, CBOC, or Vet Center, visit www2.va.gov/directory/guide/division_flsh.asp?dnum=1.

Helping Your Veteran Make the Most of His or Her Benefits

Get all the help you need from the VA and talk to others who have been there/done that. (Ravi)

If your veteran lives in an area where a variety of health care options are available, he or she may not know which way to turn. How do you and your veteran make sense of the "competing" VHA programs that he or she may be eligible for? How do you determine which programs may be best? It may help to consult with a trusted VHA or Vet Center staff member about which programs have good reputations and would be a good fit for your veteran and his or her needs. Here are some questions for you or your veteran to ask program representatives:

- "Who are the program's clients?"
- "What specific services does the program provide?"

- "Are participants satisfied with the program? Do they see results?"
- "Is there an evaluation process that rates the quality of the program?"

While various mental health resources and services are available through the VHA, some veterans with mental health concerns will never set foot in any of these clinics, for a variety of reasons, including:

- Stigma and fear of appearing weak, given the military mindset, especially when other veterans may see them seeking services
- Concerns about confidentiality

  For example, members of the Reserves or National Guard may worry that what a VHA mental health professional writes about them in their medical chart will jeopardize their military career, chance of promotion, or security clearance. Veterans may be similarly suspicious that mental health notes in their medical records might somehow be used against them, affecting, for example, a law enforcement career.
- Inaccessibility of VHA services especially in certain rural communities
- Overall disdain for any military or VA assistance by veterans who have developed a negative view of their military experience and no longer want any affiliation with military or government agencies

The VHA is aware of the reluctance, or even resistance, of some veterans toward receiving mental health care and has developed innovative programs to help with this problem. For example, the VHA now has integrated health care clinics that embed mental health care experts (usually psychologists, social workers, or psychiatric nurses) within medical clinics. This allows veterans to obtain mental health services in the context of a medical appointment, helping destigmatize the process of asking for and receiving help with a mental health issue. If you're concerned about your veteran's mental health and considering whether to encourage him or her to seek help, please review the section "When Your Veteran Doesn't Want Your Help," below.

Community Providers

For a variety of reasons including those mentioned above, some veterans and their family members seek medical and counseling services in non-VA settings like community clinics, private practice offices, civilian hospitals, or campus counseling centers. In addition, there are community organizations throughout the United States that provide pro bono (free) counseling as well as other services such as massage therapy and acupuncture. Examples are the national organization Give an Hour and regional organizations such as Los Angeles's The Soldiers Project, Boston's So Far, the San Francisco Bay Area's Coming Home Project, and Oregon's Returning Veterans Project, all of which provide various forms of support to active-duty military personnel, veterans, and their families. You can help your service member connect with these pro bono services using the list of resources at the end of this book, and you may want to consider making use of them yourself as well.

Choosing and Communicating with Your Veteran's Treatment Provider

If your veteran or other family members choose to receive mental health care from a community-based organization, we recommend "interviewing" potential mental health care providers to ask about their experience helping veterans or veterans' families. A qualified professional will be one who is culturally sensitive, knowledgeable, and competent in addressing issues faced by veterans and their families. We encourage you to read chapter 3 of our first *Courage After Fire* book, which contains a detailed section on how to select a good mental health professional.

In addition, while evidence-based treatments and cultural sensitivity are important to effective mental health care, so is the relationship your service member has (and possibly the relationship you have) with his or her provider. If you know your veteran is receiving care for mental health concerns, open up a dialogue with him or her without making any judgments and ask how you might be supportive. Could you meet the therapist or treatment team or have a phone appointment to learn more about your veteran's condition and how you can help? It can be extremely beneficial to have a joint or family session in which you meet with his or her therapist or treatment team and learn about what he or she is experiencing. You can also learn about the type of treatment being provided, as well as ways to best support your service member's recovery. If your veteran is not amenable to your meeting or speaking with the therapist, ask him or her for details of the problems and treatment so that you might learn more by reading about them.

Additionally, ask what information he or she has communicated to providers about his or her mental health problems. It's not unusual for veterans to downplay or minimize their symptoms, which unfortunately makes it harder for their providers to give the right kind of help. Mental health care providers won't typically solicit a parent's perspective, and your veteran won't necessarily think to suggest it. But if you are living with or are in close communication with your veteran, you may have critical health information that his providers don't, such as regarding medical history or behavior changes. Inquire whether he or she has fully discussed his or her health information with providers—if not, strongly encourage it. Or ask whether you can attend or call in to an appointment so you can share this health information. If your request is refused, consider writing down your concerns for your veteran to take to his or her providers.

For a number of reasons, you may not know all the health issues that your veteran is dealing with, or your veteran simply may not want you involved in his or her medical care. As difficult as this may be for you to accept, your best move may then be to encourage the person with whom your veteran feels most comfortable in a supporting role—usually his or her partner (e.g., spouse)—to share critical information with the treatment team. In emergency situations, however, it may be critical for you to make a member of the treatment team aware of your concerns. For example, if your son discloses that he has thoughts of harming himself but denies any immediate plan of acting on these thoughts, you should call his provider with this information. Remember, though, unlike your son, you are not considered the patient in this case and do not have the right to confidentiality. Hence, your son will most likely know that you contacted a member of his treatment team. But don't let this stop you from making an important call that may help and potentially save your son. In addition to calling his provider, you may also find it helpful to call the confidential National Suicide Prevention Lifeline at 1-800-273-8255 (Press "1" for the Veterans Crisis Line). If your service member is *actively* suicidal or homicidal (has an immediate plan and intent), *take him or her to the nearest emergency room or call 911.* For more information about how to assist a service member who may be suicidal, please see the end of chapter 3.

Helping Your Veteran Advocate for Care

> *My greatest concern is that I have heard that many of the physical and mental health care facilities are overloaded and the wait is too long for the urgent care that is needed.* (Erin)

It should come as no surprise if there are times when your veteran disagrees with his or her providers about the type or frequency of care needed. For example, a treatment provider may think your daughter needs to address an addiction prior to addressing the post-traumatic stress for which she is seeking help. Or maybe there is a disagreement regarding what kind of (or how much) medication to prescribe for a particular problem. So what should your veteran do if he or she disagrees with the recommendations of a provider or has a complaint about his or her treatment? Your veteran has (and you, as a family member, have) more influence on his or her care than you might think.

Here are some general guidelines to help your veteran advocate for himself or herself. While our focus is on mental health care, these same suggestions apply if your veteran is having difficulties with medical providers. Although we have written the following as a progression of steps, how *you* proceed will be determined by many factors, including what approach you choose as well as the policies and procedures of the medical center or community provider.

Have a meeting with the provider or treatment team. Encourage your veteran to meet with his or her providers or treatment team to discuss the treatment plan. If you don't think your veteran can adequately express his or her concerns about the treatment plan, then ask whether you (or your veteran's spouse) can attend or possibly call in to the appointment. If you are able to join the meeting, ask questions and voice your concerns about the treatment. Because a meeting like this can provoke anxiety for patients and family members alike, organize your thoughts prior to the meeting by making a list of your concerns and questions. Consider the following goals:

- **Get on the same page.** Ask the treatment provider to discuss the history of treatment so everyone can have the same understanding regarding the decisions about the current treatment plan.
- **Be concrete.** If you have a complaint about your veteran's treatment, provide specific dates of service with a description of what happened.
- **Be clear.** Identify how your knowledge and perspective of your veteran could be used to improve the treatment plan.

If your veteran and his or her providers can't come to an agreement on the care being provided, or if you believe that his or her complaints have not been adequately addressed, don't give up. There are still many options available to you.

Contact a supervisor. If receiving treatment through the VHA, your veteran can ask to speak with the unit chief or clinical manager, essentially the person or persons to whom the team reports. If receiving services through a community clinic or hospital, your veteran may ask to speak with the clinical director or the provider's supervisor. (As a parent, you may do the same, but we recommend you have your veteran's permission.)

Contact the patient advocate. Typically every medical center has a patient advocate, whose job is to help patients and family members resolve complaints about care. The patient advocate will help present your veteran's concerns to his or her provider(s) and attempt to resolve any issues.

Speak with the OEF/OIF/OND Case Manager. Veterans who served in Iraq or Afghanistan are assigned a case manager at the VHA hospital in which they enroll for benefits. The case manager's role is to help coordinate these veterans' entry into care and troubleshoot any problems that arise while they are receiving care. The case manager may be another person your veteran could turn to if he or she has complaints or concerns about his or her care.

Request a change in providers or a second opinion. While some treatment facilities and organizations will give alternative provider options even without a patient's asking, other facilities are reluctant to offer or advertise this as a possibility. Remember that not every provider works well with every patient; sometimes a change in providers is all that is needed for an improvement in care. One option is to ask for a second opinion within the medical center. Alternatively, those who can afford it can obtain an outside second opinion. Your veteran should request his or her medical records in order that this outside provider can review them prior to making any recommendations regarding treatment. Sometimes hearing even the same recommendations from a different provider can make a difference to your veteran.

Contact the hospital director. Speaking with the hospital director or his or her representative is also an avenue for your veteran to voice concerns. While some directors are more hands-on and interested in having someone from their office handle these complaints, others are not and will refer you back to the patient advocate.

In some cases, or if all else fails, you might voice a complaint in one of the following ways:

- Contact the Joint Commission on hospital accreditation. Visit www.jointcommission.org/report_a_complaint.aspx.
- Contact the VA Office of Inspector General (OIG). Visit www.va.gov/oig/contact/default.asp.
- Contact your US senator or representative (for tips, see www.ehow.com/how_2265620_send-complaint-letter-politician.htm).

When Your Veteran Won't Speak Up

There may be times when your veteran either is unwilling or just doesn't think to communicate specific needs or complaints about his or her treatment. It could be that he or she doesn't want to come across as a complainer or doesn't know that he or she isn't receiving the most effective treatment possible. In these instances, you or other family members may have to voice problems or concerns on your veteran's behalf.

This isn't always easy, however. Your veteran and his or her family members (including you) may not always agree on the treatment plan, and there may even be disagreement among family members about what would be helpful. In these instances, seeking assistance from a case manager or mental health provider assigned to your veteran's treatment team may help. This professional can ask all interested parties to attend a family meeting where they can voice their differing views and work together to come up with a solution that is in the veteran's best interest.

When Your Veteran Doesn't Want Your Help

At times your veteran may need your help but be too proud, ashamed, or troubled to ask. Your veteran may fear you will judge him or her as inadequate, weak, or failing. Sometimes veterans simply have little to no interest in hearing their parents' opinions or ideas about what they should do. Developmentally this makes sense: they are adults and need to make their own decisions. While rejection of an offer of help may hurt your feelings, you can take pride in your veteran's effort to make it on his or her own, which demonstrates maturity and strength. Here are some tips for helping your veteran under these circumstances.

First, recognize that your veteran's well-being doesn't and shouldn't always have to fall on your shoulders. A good question to ask yourself is *Am I the best person to talk with my veteran about these issues?* Review your veteran's social supports to determine whether someone else may be the best one to raise some or all of your areas of concern. It may be that your partner, your veteran's partner, your veteran's best friend, an uncle, or a sibling has more influence over your veteran's decisions than you do.

If you determine you are the best person to discuss an issue with your veteran, think about what you will do and say. Create a comfortable environment within which to have a conversation, and focus on the issues that concern you. Then develop a conversation that will allow the two of you to examine how "trouble areas" are progressing. Try something like: **"How do you think things are going with the VA care you are receiving?...So you don't think it's going so well? What's the next step that you need to take in order to make it go better, and how can I help you?"** Do your best to express your concern without becoming visibly upset, in order to avoid creating an adversarial relationship.

You can also consider providing information to your veteran or to his or her support system (e.g., spouse) in a more subtle way, one that influences him or her to do some research or thinking in a particular area. For example: **"Hey, I just heard about this program that might work for you.**

Here's the link," or **"I left a note on your desk about a new treatment for post-traumatic stress."** Don't get upset if your veteran doesn't welcome your ideas with open arms.

Finally, try building a team of information experts who can work together to suggest ways for your veteran to get the assistance he or she needs and deserves—this collaborative spirit can make all the difference in easing the transition from deployment and helping your veteran navigate the maze of health care options. Keep in mind that information experts may come from a variety of disciplines and backgrounds. Any of the following can be information experts:

- Relatives, friends of the family, or neighbors
- Clergy, chaplains, or spiritual leaders
- Your colleagues or your veteran's coworkers
- Case Managers or other VHA clinicians
- Other service members/veterans/veteran leaders/ community activists
- Vocational rehabilitation specialists/counselors trained to help veterans
- Veteran benefits counselors who help service members apply for a service-connected disability or pension

---

Conclusion

After deployment, or after separation or medical retirement from military service, your veteran may be eligible for a number of health care services. Determining what programs are available and which ones make sense for him or her can be a complicated yet worthwhile endeavor. It's not only the fit of the program that matters: it's how the health care providers within the program fit with your son or daughter. Consequently, a program that looks perfect "on paper" may not match your veteran's personality and needs in reality, while another program may end up working well because of the trusting relationship your son or daughter establishes with the providers involved. Your veteran deserves to use the mental health care options he or she has earned, whether at a VHA Medical Center, at a Vet Center, or through a community pro bono organization. Encourage your son or daughter to take advantage of these services—nobody merits them more!

Chapter Tips

- Help your veteran enroll in the VHA as soon as he or she is eligible.
- Recommend to your veteran that he or she get to know the layout of the local VHA facility.
- Discuss with your veteran the pros and cons of obtaining mental health support through the various options, as well as how to seek it.
- Encourage your veteran to advocate for himself or herself in order to receive the best care possible.
- You may not be the best person to help your veteran with health care decisions. Don't hesitate to organize a support team that can provide expert guidance to both your veteran and you.
- For some suggested sources of further information and support, turn to the list of resources at the back of the book.

chapter 6

Strengthening and Maintaining Relationships within Your Family

My relationship with my son is good, but other family relationships are strained somewhat because of his choice to serve. (Maria)

When a service member deploys, relationships among family members are forever changed. Mothers and fathers in particular devote tremendous amounts of time, thought, and resources to providing support to their military son or daughter, both during and after deployment.

But while you may now rejoice in your service member's long-awaited return, other family relationships may undergo additional stress as you tend to your service member and the challenges of readjustment. If your service member sustained psychological or physical injuries, you may find it especially difficult to focus on the needs of other family members. Maybe you assume that these other relationships—with your partner (e.g., spouse), your service member's siblings, your service member's partner, or your own parents—will operate on autopilot while you focus on the needs of your service member. However, each of these relationships requires care and attention to maintain the overall strength of your family.

The purpose of this chapter is to highlight how relationships among family members may be affected by deployment and how they may change even further after deployment. To this end, we'll outline strategies to help you enhance or strengthen your family, and we'll also provide suggestions to help you repair relationships that may have suffered. Finally, we'll suggest conversation starters to aid you in discussing concerns with other family members, and we'll offer tips for rebuilding relationships. You may find that the strategies we suggest for use in a certain type of relationship may also be applied in your other relationships. While we cannot cover every possible relationship concern, our hope is that you'll find this chapter relevant and useful regardless of the size, configuration, and complexity of your family.

Family Structure

Let's begin with a discussion of how families work in general, so you can determine what needs to be done to strengthen your family now that your service member has returned. According to the eminent psychiatrist Salvador Minuchin (1974), in order to function well all families need a certain amount of structure, order, and routine. In every family, individuals take on, or are placed in, certain roles. Sometimes these roles are welcomed, while at other times they are a burden to the individual or to the family.

The particular roles that family members take on interact with and are reinforced by the roles that other family members assume. This dynamic can be simple and supportive, such as when one person cooks and another cleans up; or difficult and distressing, such as when one person tends to criticize and another responds defensively. Whatever the roles, over time, these patterns become ingrained and typically become more complicated as more family members are added.

Before your service member deployed, he or she probably helped out around the house. Maybe he or she regularly mowed the lawn, cooked meals on Thursday nights, babysat for younger siblings, and took out the garbage. Your service member may have played an important role as well in the psychological well-being of your family—for example, as the "peacemaker" when conflicts arose or as a younger sibling's mentor and confidant. So when your service member deployed, some reorganization of your family structure most likely took place. Even if your service member didn't live with you prior to deployment, your family may still have had to make adjustments in order to function optimally when he or she was deployed. For instance, before going off to war, maybe your service member was a valuable source of advice for siblings even when he or she lived in another state, or perhaps your service member called you every Sunday evening to keep you apprised of what was going on in his or her life.

Because parents experience the absence of a service member from the "family unit" in different ways, they adapt with a multitude of strategies and rearrange the family structure accordingly. While some parents put many of the things that their service member was responsible for on hold, waiting for him or her to return and pick up his or her normal "duties," others reassign these duties or take them on themselves. For example, when your service member was deployed, maybe a younger sibling took out the garbage or walked the dog, or maybe you found yourself mowing the lawn for the first time in years. You may even have welcomed your service member's partner into your home or spent significant time looking after your grandchildren. These and other role changes can greatly strain family relationships.

It may have taken a while for everyone to adjust to their new roles. And perhaps just when you all were finally getting used to things, your service member returned from deployment, spurring another round of adjustment, with everyone struggling once again to determine their place in the family structure. This can be particularly true if your service member is having difficulty reintegrating or is suffering from physical or psychological injuries. Even if your service member did not live with you prior to deployment and is not living with you now, you may struggle just as much, not knowing what role you should play during his or her readjustment. You may find it especially challenging at times when your service member is noncommunicative or avoids family gatherings, leading you to feel anxious and in the dark about how he or she is really doing.

Connection: Something We All Need

As much as you worked to adjust to a new family structure during your service member's absence, your energy and thoughts may still have been primarily focused on him or her. It's not uncommon during deployment for parents to be constantly concerned and anxiously counting the days until their service member's return. Yet this preoccupation may have hampered your ability to give attention to those around you, making it difficult for you to see how your partner or your other children were affected by your service member's absence and potentially damaging your bonds with them and other loved ones.

Now that your service member has returned, you can begin to consider and address the ways in which the bonds within your family were affected by his or her deployment. According to attachment experts John Bowlby (1988) and Sue Johnson (2004), we all need loving relationships and connections with family and friends in order to thrive. Our need for attachment or bonding is biologically driven and helps us feel both safe and secure, which in turn allows us to function more effectively in our families and in the world.

While your service member was overseas, he or she probably developed a very strong attachment to fellow service members who all shared life-changing experiences and protected one another from harm. Further, when people are exposed to immediate threat, they form very close relationships more quickly, so your service member may have forged especially intense bonds with battle buddies. Indeed, your service member may feel torn by intense loyalty to both his or her "military family" and his or her actual family, which can make readjustment quite challenging.

As your service member's relationships and connections shifted and changed in importance while he or she was deployed, so may have yours at home. Perhaps worrying about your daughter's safety brought you and your partner closer together—on the other hand, perhaps it proved too much for the relationship to bear. If you were already divorced or separated from your service member's other parent, maybe your ex-partner stepped up and helped out in surprising ways. Maybe one of your service member's younger siblings suddenly matured and took on extra responsibilities. These changes may have strengthened certain connections as you discovered that you could lean on other family members and relate to one another in new ways. On the other hand, such shifts may have resulted in significant challenges for you and placed new and different kinds of stress on the whole family. This stress may even have actually increased once your service member came home. Thus, the idea of now creating a sense of family "togetherness" can feel challenging, overwhelming, or even impossible.

Partners May Have Different Ways of Coping

> *[To those who have never had a son or daughter deploy] Do not tell us how hard your life is since your kid went to college or moved out of the country.* (Justin)

Before we consider some common shifts and strains that occur within families during and after deployment, take a moment to recall what it was like when your child first left the "nest" for whatever reason—college, marriage, the military, or other circumstances. As you know, it's not unusual for parents to feel anxious about their child's well-being when he or she leaves the family home. But when that child leaves to enter military service and then deploys, the level of anxiety is understandably higher than if he or she were, say, going off to college. Whether he or she is leaving home for the first time or moved out years ago, the stress of having a son or daughter deploy can increase your need for connection with other important people in your life—loved ones who share your concern and whom you can turn to for support, like your partner.

However, if you and your partner were both overly focused on your service member's well-being while he or she was deployed, you may have inadvertently neglected to care for each other and consequently may have exacerbated difficulties or sore points that already existed between you. Perhaps the two of you managed the stress of deployment differently and are also handling the homecoming in separate ways. Some parents throw themselves into work or other activities as a way to cope with deployment; others desperately look to discuss their concerns about their service member's safety and later readjustment. Perhaps you or your partner wants to talk about how your service member seems "changed," but the other wants to avoid these discussions at all costs to keep from feeling worried or upset. While the refusal to talk can be interpreted as uncaring or dismissive, maybe even cold, by the parent who wants to share his or her concerns, the avoidant parent may see the other parent as needy or obsessed and feel pressured to "fix" the problem without knowing how. Feeling helpless and frustrated, the avoidant parent may subsequently spend even more time at work, sidestepping all opportunities to talk about anything having to do with the returned service member, which in turn increases the tension at home.

Ironically, while both of you are reacting to the same stressful situation and may even have similar concerns, in this situation you are each managing your stress in very different ways, leading to disconnection, misunderstandings, or arguments. You may disagree about a variety of things, but it all stems from the same anxiety or fear: your son or daughter has returned from war and is having difficulty readjusting. Neither of these coping strategies (talking or not talking) is more adaptive or better than the other—they're just different. The communication difficulties or feelings of disconnection between you and your partner may be new, or they may reflect long-standing conflicts reignited by stress.

Partner Relationships

Jared has been living with his parents, Sarah and Jim (married twenty-six years), since returning from Iraq six weeks ago. He spends most of the time in his room watching TV or playing video games. Deep inside, Sarah is worried that he is having a hard time and is withdrawing from the world, but rather than specifically addressing these issues with him, she communicates her concerns with demands that he clean up his room and participate in family functions. Jared's response is to shut down and withdraw from her and the rest of the family even further. Feeling rejected, Sarah anxiously approaches Jim to discuss her worries. He thinks Jared just needs time and space to "move forward" and dismisses Sarah's concerns by telling her that "everything will be fine." This leaves her feeling more worried and rejected—as if she has no one to talk to. Sarah then begins to criticize Jim, telling him that he hasn't been around enough to know that their son is having a difficult time, leading Jim to quietly withdraw, unsure of what to say or do.

Many times, especially when the health and safety of a child is at stake, communication between parents can be problematic and unproductive. What if Jim had responded by sitting down and listening to Sarah instead of dismissing her worries? He may have been swayed by her concerns and helped her devise a plan to communicate these concerns to their son. On the other hand, after listening to Sarah, he may have disagreed and presented her with reasons why he did not share her concerns. In either case, responding with empathy would have helped Sarah feel heard and validated, allowing her to feel more connected to Jim. Instead, as Sarah's anxiety mounted, she began to pressure Jim to "do something," when what she needed most in that moment was comfort and understanding. Overwhelmed by Sarah's distress, Jim put more distance between them, further straining their marriage. Alternatively, if Sarah had approached Jim by emphasizing how important he was to her, she would probably have found him more willing and able to listen and ease her worries about their son.

How to Reconnect

How do you and your partner deal with differences in the way you manage stress? How can you begin to break down the emotional wall, now that your son or daughter has come home? How can you identify and better meet your partner's needs?

Below are steps for having healthy, successful conversations about the effect of your service member's deployment and reintegration on your relationship with your partner. These steps include strategies to help you understand how you and your partner each communicate and to help you identify ways you can satisfy each other's need to connect. Note that the guidelines and conversation starters in these steps can be used to improve the bond between you and your partner even if your relationship is still strong. Remember: the stronger your relationship, the better you'll be able to help your son or daughter. Many of the principles contained in these steps can also be put to use in your other significant relationships to strengthen your connections with family members and friends.

Step 1: Make a commitment. To improve on your current communication style, it's important that you and your partner each agree with the statements below and can commit to being guided by them in order to facilitate productive conversations:

- I am committed to helping our son or daughter and believe that doing so will improve our relationship.
- I am willing to talk with my partner about my concerns.
- I am interested in feeling more connected to my partner and would like to better understand how our son or daughter's deployment and reintegration has affected him or her.

- I believe my partner is interested in becoming more connected with me and would like to better understand how our son or daughter's deployment and reintegration has affected me.
- I am interested in finding new ways to improve our relationship.
- I will be accountable for my words and actions.
- I am willing to risk being vulnerable with my partner because he or she is important to me, and I know we both have the same goal: to help our son/daughter readjust.

In addition, if your emotions or your partner's emotions tend to escalate quickly, we recommend that you both commit to not using alcohol or drugs before or during your conversations, to decrease the likelihood of saying or doing anything that you might regret. Remember, habits you may have developed while your service member was deployed can be contributing to the difficulties you are experiencing. For example, poor sleep, poor eating habits, or excessive alcohol use can lead to problematic communication with loved ones, including your partner. You may first need to address such negative behaviors in order to improve communication. We provide recommendations for addressing these unhealthy habits in chapter 1 and tips for positive coping in chapter 7.

If you and your partner are able to approach each other with this set of guidelines in mind, your conversations are much more likely to be successful (i.e., both of you will have the opportunity to be heard and feel understood and respected). If either you or your partner doesn't agree with one or more of the preceding principles, discuss why not. You may find that your relationship could benefit from couples therapy. If you no longer have the ability or desire to improve your relationship, you might consider the guidelines later in this chapter for separated or divorced parents.

Step 2: Stop the "dance" and work together. Often people develop problematic interactional patterns with their partner in failed attempts at a better connection, especially during times of stress. Identifying how interactions with your partner tend to "play out" is critical to establishing a new set of more useful interactions. If you can identify your interactional pattern or "dance," then you and your partner can work to improve it instead of having it divide you.

It may be easy to see what your *partner* is doing that is problematic but much harder to see how *you* might be contributing to any difficulties. Try to see how your partner's behavior "fits" with and reinforces your reactions and how your behavior encourages your partner's reactions. Make observations. For example, sharing the realization "The more I push to talk about our son, the more you push for space" can be really useful. If you identify the *pattern*—not your partner—as the problem, it decreases the likelihood that your partner will feel as if you are blaming him or her for the conflict, which often leads to defensive posturing and builds resentment.

Let's take the earlier example of Sarah and Jim. When these two have a disagreement, Sarah typically attempts to connect with Jim by making demands of him. However, when Jim is unsure of how to help, he chooses to withdraw because he's concerned that he may make matters worse by intervening. If Sarah and Jim can come to see this kind of interaction as their "dance" they do again and again, then they can do something about it. For example, they can develop their own code for "We're doing that dance again—let's not do it" as a way of interrupting the potentially problematic pattern.

Step 3: Remember to be kind. It's not uncommon for partners to approach their son or daughter's readjustment from different perspectives. As we described earlier, partners may have distinct ways of coping, but it's crucial to listen to each other's perspective and not label and attack it as abnormal, wrong, or "the problem." It's easy to become critical of your partner's way of coping, especially when it's different from yours. Commenting on the inadequacy of your partner's approach will only fuel conflicts.

Developing compassion and a deeper understanding of your partner's coping style will help you maintain and potentially enhance your closeness. Learning about your partner's family history and upbringing can help you understand the origins of his or her coping strategies, which may lead you to feel more compassion and not take his or her interaction style personally. For example, knowing the difficulties your husband faced growing up in a single-parent home may allow you to see his avoidance as an inevitable result of how he was raised rather than something he is doing *to you*.

Step 4: Structure your conversation. Conversations about stressful topics tend to go more smoothly when they're planned rather than sparked by the heat of negative emotion. Together with your partner, decide on a time to talk when neither of you will be too tired or too busy to focus, and try to minimize the possibility of interruption—no phone, other family members, pets, or other distractions. Be sure to limit the length of the conversation, and plan to keep it centered on the underlying emotional issues that may be driving the conflict rather than the surface issues that appear to be causing difficulties. Anything that doesn't get covered in the allotted time can be addressed in another conversation. As with any skill, the more you practice, the easier it gets, and the less you will need to formally structure these conversations.

Step 5: Start the conversation. While each couple has its own rhythm and style of communication, here is a template for you to begin talking with your partner about the impact of your son or daughter's deployment upon your relationship. **"I'm concerned that when ______________ was gone, we grew apart. We were both concerned about ______________'s well-being and didn't talk enough. You coped your way, and I coped my way. Now that ______________ is back, I'd like for us to be able to find time to talk regularly again, to give our relationship the time it deserves so we can adjust to our new circumstances. Let's talk about our coping styles and what might be really going on for each of us."**

Conversations about emotionally laden issues can easily veer off track. If this occurs, remind yourself of the goal of the conversation, and gently redirect the conversation to the original topic.

Step 6: Ask open-ended questions. Open-ended questions (see the list below for examples), which allow for a wide variety of answers, can help you learn more about how your service member's deployment affected your partner and how that may have affected your relationship. Actively listen to your partner's responses without judging him or her, recognizing that feelings about this stressful experience can be really hard to share. Sometimes reflecting back to your partner what he or she has just said or asking for clarification—for example, "Can you say more about that?"—will help you better understand and respond to what's important.

- "How do you think our son's military service has affected our relationship?"
- "How has the way that each of us reacted to and handled our daughter's deployment affected 'us'?"
- "How is our son's return from deployment affecting 'us'?"
- "What do you see as the main problem in our relationship right now?"
- "What problems or feelings have you most been struggling with?"
- "When did these difficulties or feelings start? Have they always been there to some extent? Or did they surface after our daughter deployed?
- How might each of our family histories and past experiences relate to our relationship now?"
- "How do you think I've changed? How do you think you've changed?"
- "How can I help you?"

Step 7: Prepare to hear criticism. When you discuss your relationship with your partner and ask how your service member's deployment has affected you as a couple, your partner may respond in ways that trigger you to become defensive, become critical, or shut down. For example, you may become irritable and impatient with your wife when she makes comments that make you feel vulnerable, such as "If you cared as much as I do about our son, then you would understand" or "Why can't you face the fact that he is not doing well?" or "Why don't you do something when he is disrespectful to me?" Prepare yourself to hear criticism like this about how you've handled some aspect of the relationship. Although you may feel tempted to respond with "Can't you see I'm doing the best I can?" or "Give me a break; you have no idea what I'm going through," to do so may lead to a fight. Instead, attempt to track each of your interactional patterns, identifying the underlying need for connection driving your behaviors. First, ask yourself what your partner is really trying to tell you when he or she becomes critical or defensive or shuts down. Then consider how you can step out of your typical pattern of communicating when it's not working. For example, ask yourself how you can modify your own problematic responses so you feel closer to your partner and strengthen your relationship.

Step 8: Just breathe. Remember to pay close attention to your breathing. As you know, when your emotions are excited your breathing tends to become rapid and shallow—this causes the vessels that carry blood to your brain to constrict, making it difficult to think clearly. Come up with a strategy to remind yourself to breathe slowly from the diaphragm and to focus on extending your exhalations. This could consist of writing down a "breathing reminder" on a piece of paper or wearing a piece of jewelry or rubber band to remind you of the significance of slow and easy breathing. Instructions for a slow breathing exercise are found in chapter 7.

Step 9: Evaluate and adjust the process if necessary. Between conversations, regularly discuss how the process of having these talks is going, and be willing to change the structure or format as the two of you see fit.

Step 10: Spend time together. During the time that your service member was deployed, you may have been too preoccupied or focused on communications with him or her to spend much time with your partner. Now that your service member has returned, you may be even more distracted by concerns about his or her well-being, or if he or she has been injured you may be spending long hours providing care. While talking is one important way to improve things between you and your partner, doing physical activities or working on projects together can also provide opportunities to heal or enhance your connection. This can include going for walks, going to a place of worship, going to the movies, fixing up or remodeling part of the house, planning a vacation, sorting through and rearranging a room, gardening, going for a peaceful drive, working on a crossword puzzle, or other activities you used to enjoy but put on hold when your service member was overseas.

Jointly creating ways to commemorate or reflect on your service member's deployment—such as putting letters you saved in a scrapbook, compiling a photo album or producing a video of the past year's milestones, or preparing care packages for deployed troops your service member knows—may be especially helpful. Because time can easily pass you by when you are preoccupied by concerns about your service member, plan ahead by purposefully initiating outings and inviting your partner to participate in activities with you. If your partner declines, suggest an alternative or work together to break the activity into more manageable tasks or steps.

Strengthening a Healthy Relationship

Some couples' relationships are actually strengthened as a result of the challenges they face together during and after a son or daughter's deployment. If this applies to you, here is an example of how you can initiate a conversation to build on this strength: **"We really came together during _______________'s deployment and return home. I felt as though I could depend on you to help overcome the difficulties that we faced. This whole process allowed me to feel closer to you. How can we make sure we're able to keep the momentum going and hang on to what we've developed, to keep us strong for the future?"**

Even if you and your partner have experienced problems and conflicts in the wake of your service member's deployment, there may be aspects of your relationship that have improved or flourished. It's worthwhile to spend time in conversation identifying those aspects that are working, because this can help sustain and enhance your connection. Highlighting those moments in which you and your partner leaned on each other can reinforce and strengthen these successful patterns of interaction, providing more clarity on what to do if problems arise.

Working with Your Ex-Partner

If you are separated or divorced from your service member's other parent, love and support for your service member is probably one thing the two of you continue to have in common. Since your service member deployed, this commonality may have become particularly strong. While relationships between ex-partners obviously vary, we recommend you now make working together to respond to your service member's needs a priority.

So how do you and your ex-partner have an effective conversation about your service member? How can you communicate in ways that will allow you both to assist your son or daughter in the best way possible?

Keeping in mind complicating factors that may bleed into your relationship with your ex-partner (including the fact that you may not like his or her new partner), we recommend the following guidelines to help you work with, rather than against, each other during this often rocky phase:

- Prior to talking with your ex-partner, write down what you hope to accomplish in your conversation.

- State your concerns to your ex-partner clearly and succinctly.

- Keep the conversation focused on those tasks you both want to accomplish that will help your service member.

- Communicate your concerns in the form of "I" statements rather than "You" statements. Be sure to keep your service member as the focus of the conversation rather than focusing on your ex-partner's behavior. For example, "I'm concerned about how our son is doing" is better than "You aren't handling things well with our son."

- Be aware of your own triggers or issues that have the potential to lead you to overreact. These may include sensitive issues related to your breakup, your new partner, or your ex's new partner. These conversations, if not closely monitored, can become overwhelming and easily lead to old, familiar, but unproductive patterns of interacting.

Tips for Especially Challenging "Ex" Relationships

If your relationship with your ex-partner is too far gone to repair, or if there is yelling or fighting much of the time, limit your contact and communicate as much as possible by e-mail, text, or phone rather than in person. If you need to meet with your ex-partner, do so in a public place, perhaps accompanied by a friend.

Not all former relationships can be repaired enough to facilitate civil conversations. If your ex-partner has a significant history of physical or verbal abuse and you haven't felt safe enough to successfully have a conversation with him or her, discontinue interactions altogether and only deal directly with your service member.

Remember that the goal is to provide optimal support to your service member, which you can do only if you maximize your safety and minimize your stress.

Sibling Relationships

Brandina, the younger sister of Jorge—an Iraq and Afghanistan veteran—told her mother: "I'm not sure I know what it takes to get your attention these days. All you talk about is Jorge. I don't think you even know I exist."

If your service member has difficulty readjusting, it can place stress on you and the entire family. As a result, your service member's siblings may need you more, while you may feel as if you have less to give. Even though brothers and sisters may feel tremendous pride in their military sibling, they can also have a range of other emotions and concerns, especially if they think that you have given or currently give their military sibling more attention, as Brandina expresses above.

Nonmilitary Siblings

Here is a sampling of the emotions nonmilitary siblings may feel:

- They may feel neglected and hurt by you for not understanding or meeting their needs.
- They may feel jealous of or angry at their military sibling for receiving more attention and worry that they "don't count" or are less important in your eyes.
- They may feel insignificant or as if their concerns are unimportant compared to what their military sibling experienced while deployed or the difficulties that he or she is now facing.
- They may feel conflicted, even guilty, about discussing their problems with you for fear of burdening you even more.
- They may feel upset at their military sibling for having "abandoned" them when he or she went off to war, leaving them to grow up on their own or deal with family issues stateside.
- They may feel irritated that their military sibling seems "lazy" and isn't trying harder to get better.
- They may deny that there is anything wrong at all with their military sibling and defend him or her to you when you express concern.

They may respond with a host of reactions as well, such as:

- Acting out or attempting to get attention from you in negative ways

  Negative behaviors can include experimenting with smoking, drugs, or alcohol; promiscuity; spending excessive time on the Internet and/or playing video games; withdrawing from family activities; neglecting hygiene and appearance; performing poorly in school or at work; or displaying an overall disrespectful attitude toward you.

- Trying extra hard to please you by showing positive behavior, like doing well in school, at work, or in sports

  If such attempts to get your attention are not successful, nonmilitary siblings may become increasingly depressed or angry.

- Spending more time with friends, coming to depend more on them than on you for support

- Developing strong political opinions that are contrary to yours or your service member's

Military Siblings

Two siblings who both have served in the military may have a deep and profound understanding of each other and their military experiences. This shared insight may bring comfort to them in a way that no other family member can. They can be quick to stick up for each other and to deny any difficulties that the other is having because it hits too close to home or because they intimately understand what he or she is going through. One sibling also can end up being the "translator" for the other to share information about how he or she is doing with the rest of the family.

Be aware, however, that while the bond of military service may bridge a gap of understanding that is too vast for others to cross, it's also possible that siblings' military experiences are significantly different; consequently they may misinterpret each other's feelings or reactions.

Tips for Talking with Your Children

My older son is sensitive to the attention his brother receives and the time that I spend involved in activities that support his younger brother. I have had to make sure that I don't neglect my nonmilitary son and his life while I worry and am quite preoccupied with my younger son's situation. (Tury)

Any of your service member's siblings who haven't served in the military may be wrestling with all sorts of reactions and acting out to get your attention, as we described above. Yet your nonmilitary son or daughter can have great trouble directly expressing his or her needs or concerns to you. So how do you begin to have a conversation about these important issues? The type of conversation you have will be determined by a number of factors, including the age of your nonmilitary son or daughter and what has been historically the most successful way to communicate with him or her. Your goals for the conversation will also vary, from educating your son or daughter about the issues his or her military sibling faces to providing him or her with the attention and connection felt to have been lacking. Perhaps an informal, low-key approach such as "walking and talking" or having a series of brief, unstructured conversations—maybe even while you're doing an activity together—will work well and allow your nonmilitary son or daughter to see that you are able to continue to provide support even though you are concerned about your service member.

On the other hand, some parents prefer to use a more structured, formal process of addressing these issues. If this is the case for you, it's important to structure the talk in such a way that your son or daughter will feel safe to express feelings and not be criticized or misunderstood. Therefore, try to make the conversation not too rigid or stuffy.

Whether you use an informal or a formal approach with your service member's nonmilitary sibling, here are some tips to help you prepare:

- Determine whether such conversations are best had with the entire family (if there are additional siblings) or with each individual sibling.

- Involve your partner in the planning of the conversation, including the decision as to whether you both will participate.

- Be mindful that nonmilitary siblings may be afraid of, or even dread, these conversations because they feel as if they are burdening you or not deserving of your attention. In your conversation, acknowledge and validate their feelings and let them know how much you care for them.

- Recognize that nonmilitary siblings may deny any problem or claim that *you* are the problem. If this happens, don't become defensive. Validate and empathize with their perspective while gently educating them regarding the issues faced by their military sibling.

- Plan to use a nonjudgmental tone and neutral body language.

- Consider the following introductions and select one as a possible template for initiating a conversation:

  "I know I have placed a lot of my attention on your brother since he was deployed and also now that he has returned home, but I want you to know how much you mean to me. I really want to hear how you are doing and have you tell me how I can better give you what you need from now on. Please don't be concerned that what you tell me will add to my stress."

  "You and I may see things differently regarding how we can best help your brother. I want to hear your thoughts about this. At the end of the conversation, we may not entirely agree, but your opinions and ideas are important to me, because you are important to me."

Another way to start a conversation with a military sibling might be **"I know you handled your service in**

ways both similar to and different from your brother. You have an expertise on this experience that I don't. Can you help me understand what he is going through and how I might be able to help him readjust?"

Sibling Strains

[My military son's siblings] felt I loved him more. My youngest daughter doesn't talk to me. (Rachel)

Earlier in this chapter, we discussed how your service member's absence and subsequent return home can upend family structure and roles. Let's consider more closely the relationship between a service member and his or her sibling. While this relationship may have been on hold or dormant while your service member was deployed, with neither really knowing the changes taking place in the other, now that your service member is back, the nature of the relationship may be transformed. After deployment, some service members come to fill a parental role for their siblings, while in some families the opposite happens. In some cases, because they feel significantly more mature due to their experience, those who have deployed become bossy toward or overly protective of their siblings, even older ones. This upsets family dynamics. In these types of circumstances, your children may need help from you to maintain supportive and healthy relationships with one another.

As an example, let's discuss the returning service member who jumps into a parental role and attempts to provide guidance to his or her siblings. In some families, this guidance can be incredibly helpful, while in others it exacerbates difficulties between siblings. This is especially true if a younger sibling who went off to war now wants to provide his or her older sibling with advice (usurping the older sibling's traditional role). The following is a starter for a conversation with your returning service member about his or her relationships with the rest of the family (in this example, specifically a sister): **"We've really missed your input in the family. I know that you are concerned about your sister and want to do what**

you can in order to help her along. What can I do to help you figure out how you can best help her?"

Watch for changes in siblings' roles and dynamics, especially if your service member returned with a significant disability. Although concern and caring for an injured sibling is admirable, it can also lead siblings to neglect their own goals or aspirations in the service of the one who was wounded. If this seems to be happening in your family, you may need to discuss it with your service member's sibling. Ask whether he or she is really taking on this role by choice and not just because there seems no other option or because he or she is trying to please you or get your love and attention. Consider starting your conversation like this: **"I know that you have been very worried about your injured brother since he returned. I really appreciate your concern for him. I'm afraid that in your efforts to take care of him you may lose yourself or lose track of your own needs and life goals. How can we make sure this doesn't happen?"**

Strains with Your Service Member's Partner

During their son Thomas's deployment, his parents Brenda and Marcus provided his wife, Joyce—a veteran herself—with financial help and made numerous offers to take care of their grandchildren. Joyce initially accepted this help but subsequently turned them down, offering no explanation. Since then, relations have been strained. Thomas returned from deployment two months ago, but Brenda and Marcus haven't had an opportunity to spend time with him, Joyce, or their grandchildren. They feel excluded, as if they don't matter anymore to their son or his family. It's not because Thomas has been too busy catching up with his wife and children—he has been spending long hours on the computer, checking in on his buddies who are still deployed. Even Joyce feels disconnected from him.

Whether you and your service member's partner (e.g., spouse) are currently close or distant likely depends on how you interacted before, during, and after your service member's deployment. Many other factors can affect how you feel toward your service member's partner and what type of relationship you have. For instance, often partners of service members have also served in the military and therefore can relate exceptionally well to the post-deployment readjustment experience. This can play out positively, as such a partner may be extremely supportive to your service member and also help "translate" or make sense of his or her behavior for you. In the scenario above, however, we see how two parents' strained relationship with their daughter-in-law drives a wedge between them and their military son.

Since returning to the states, your service member may be experiencing a challenging three-way loyalty split: feeling attachment to (1) his or her original family (parents, siblings, etc.), (2) the family he or she has created (e.g., partner and children), and (3) his or her "military family" (the troops with whom he or she served). Thomas, in the case above, is a perfect example. Even though you were "first" as parents, you may have been relegated to third place on the list of people to stay in contact or spend time with. It's normal to have a strong reaction to this perceived slight, as Brenda and Marcus did, including feeling annoyed, hurt, angry, disappointed, or even jealous of the relationship your service member has with his or her partner.

> *Things get tough with my daughter-in-law; she and I have a roller-coaster relationship.* (Melissa)

Your issues with your son or daughter's partner can be compounded if you have never enjoyed a good relationship with this individual or think that this individual is doing a poor job of managing the household, handling financial responsibilities, taking care of your grandchildren, or tending to your service member's needs or other family matters. Having issues with your son or daughter's choice of partner can pose difficulties in any situation, but it can be especially challenging if you have great concern about your service member or grandchildren's emotional or physical well-being and think that the decision to marry or be partnered with this person was impulsive or driven by the wrong reasons. If it feels as if there is a never-ending tug-of-war between you and your service member's partner, here are some tools to help you begin to manage this tension:

- Practice saying (rehearsing) one of the statements below to yourself so it becomes your mantra when your emotions run high in response to something your service member's partner says or does. (This is an example of "self-talk," which we discuss in chapter 7.)
    - *I'm on the same team as ______________, and we both want to help my daughter successfully readjust to life in the states.*
    - *I'm grateful my son is home, and I want to work with ______________ to make sure that he is okay.*
    - *I can control how I react to ______________ even if I believe she is not the best partner for my son.*
- Compliment or give positive feedback to your service member's partner for those things he or she has done well or is doing to help your service member. Be specific and genuine when you express your appreciation.
- Consider having a frank conversation with your service member's partner about how the two of you can most effectively help your service member transition to the civilian world. The last thing either one of you wants is to sabotage the other's efforts in this regard. It's important to focus on your service member's needs and not get pulled into discussing other issues, such as long-held resentments. Here is one way to start this conversation: **"Our communication hasn't always been great, and I haven't always handled things as well as I should have. But we do have something in common: we both want what is best for ______________ and for your family. How can we work together to help ____________ adjust to being home?"**

    Finally, *you* may also feel divided if you developed a close relationship with your service member's partner while he or she was deployed. If your service member is having difficulty reengaging in family relationships or not following through on caretaking or household responsibilities, you may empathize with your service member's partner and feel tempted to criticize or lash out at your service member. Remembering that your service member may be struggling with reintegration issues or suffering from psychological or physical injuries can help you respond with compassion for your service member as well as his or her partner. If you can recognize that the problem is not your service member but your service member's way of coping with post-deployment challenges, this can help you stay calm and not overreact.

Couples or Family Therapy

It's not always clear when professional help is needed in the form of couples or family therapy; however, here are some signs that family relationships are in trouble and you and your family could use additional support:

- Communication between family members often erupts into arguments or strained silence.
- You or other family members have withdrawn significantly from daily activities and family functions since your service member deployed.
- There is violent or abusive behavior (e.g., emotional or physical abuse) among family members.

In the last case, the kind of assistance needed may range from police involvement to individual therapy to couples or family therapy, depending on the circumstances under which the violence takes place as well as how frequently it occurs. We recommend that you consult with a mental health professional who has experience dealing with family violence to determine whether therapy is appropriate.

As far as what kind of couples or family therapy makes sense for you, a number of well-established family therapies have a good evidence base (i.e., research studies show they work). These include:

- Structural family therapy
- Strategic family therapy
- Functional family therapy
- Multi-family group therapy
- Emotionally focused couples therapy
- Integrative behavioral couples therapy

While an evidence-based approach is important, it's even more important that you be comfortable with your therapist and feel a sense of safety and trust with him or her. The therapist you choose should have an understanding of military families, have experience using an effective therapeutic approach, and be someone with whom you feel safe enough to discuss intimate details of your family. Remember, if you aren't able to talk freely about what is happening in your family, then you won't end up getting the help you deserve.

Conclusion

Family relationships shift when individuals go off to war, and your service member's safe return doesn't mean that the pieces of your family puzzle will fall perfectly back into place. As a result of your service member's deployment and the time and energy you invested in supporting him or her from afar, it's expected that you will experience some strains in your important relationships—such as those with your partner, your service member, your service member's partner, and your service member's siblings. At the same time, you now have a wonderful opportunity to deepen these relationships. Through honest communication and genuine appreciation for all you have borne together, you can strengthen your family bonds.

Chapter Tips

- Don't judge yourself, or anyone else, harshly for changes that have happened in your family.
- The key to success is good communication. Plan how you can have successful conversations with family members affected by your service member's deployment and readjustment.
- Be patient. Just as it can take time for your service member to readjust, it can take time for you and other family members to repair connections with one another.
- Accept that your service member may be caught in a three-way loyalty split (between you and your family, his or her own family, and his or her fellow service members), which can make reintegration challenging for everyone.
- Find ways to change the "dance" or unhealthy communication patterns and interactions between you and your partner, especially when coping with your service member's readjustment.
- Increase your connection with your partner. Remember that underneath your partner's criticism and defensiveness may be a softer, more vulnerable set of emotions that if expressed could strengthen your connection, particularly now that your service member is home.
- For some suggested sources of further information and support, turn to the list of resources at the back of the book.

Chapter Tips

chapter 7

Caring Is Wearing: Taking Good Care of Yourself to Better Help Your Service Member

> During his third tour in Iraq, Jeremy's vehicle was hit by an IED. He suffered multiple physical and psychological injuries including TBI, severed nerves in his right arm, post-traumatic stress, and depression. Jeremy was medically retired from the Marines at age twenty-four. A few months later, his girlfriend broke up with him. Jeremy's mother, Alice, quit her job in order to care for him, while her husband, Craig, picked up a second job to make up for the lost income.

As you are probably aware, supporting or caring for a service member after deployment is wearing, if not downright exhausting. In this chapter, we'll begin by briefly describing some of the ways in which the strain of supporting a son or daughter facing post-deployment challenges can negatively affect your health and well-being. Then we'll offer a self-care regimen comprising an array of strategies and skills for increasing your self-awareness and enhancing your self-care. Our goal is to help you stay as resilient as possible, keeping up your strength and stamina so you are best able to assist your service member no matter what challenges he or she faces.

Sacrifice

As mental health professionals with years of experience working with veterans of World War II through the first Gulf War, we have learned just how immense the commitment and sacrifices are that service members like yours make. But it wasn't until the recent protracted wars in Iraq and Afghanistan that we became fully aware of the sacrifices made by *parents* in support of their military sons and daughters and the toll this can take on their physical and emotional health. We also have come to understand that while certain similarities exist, each parent's experience of helping their service member is different, depending upon a constellation of variables. All of the following influence the extent to which your service member's readjustment may affect you:

- His or her age, gender, length of service, and type and number of deployments
- Whether he or she was living with or in the same community as you prior to deployment
- His or her emotional and physical health prior to deployment
- His or her post-deployment condition (e.g., the extent of physical and psychological injuries)
- The closeness of the parent-child relationship prior to deployment
- Your gender and personal background (e.g., whether you have military experience or a history of trauma)
- Your physical and emotional health
- The level of emotional and financial support you and your service member receive from family, friends, and community members

In the case of Alice and Craig above, their son's needs have propelled them back to when Jeremy was young. Alice has sacrificed her career goals to care for him and tend to his needs 24/7, while Craig works extra hours to make ends meet. As taxing as such round-the-clock parenting might have been when Jeremy was a young child, now that they are caring for an injured adult son Alice and Craig find it entirely exhausting, both physically and emotionally. Not only are they less capable of meeting the physical demands of such sustained care now that they are older, but the emotional pull to focus their energy and resources on their son and his recovery has led them to neglect their own needs. This is not uncommon for parents like Alice and Craig, who are willing to do "whatever it takes" to see their son restored to his former strength and independence or simply lessen his pain.

But while the "whatever it takes" approach may work in an emergency or acute crisis, healing and reintegration requires patience and endurance, of service members as well as their loved ones. Although intense self-sacrifice may seem an appropriate response to the emotional or physical wounds that your son or daughter received while serving, in the end it can negatively affect your well-being and in turn hinder your ability to care for him or her.

Compassion Fatigue and Secondary Traumatic Stress

When he was deployed, I felt emotionally depleted. Nothing was going on in my brain. I was not moving off the sofa.... I couldn't say his name. I woke up screaming because I swear I heard him call out to me, "Mom, Mom! Are you there?" (Judith)

Compassion is the desire to help someone who is suffering, out of sympathy. For parents, the compassion that they feel when their child—regardless of age—is struggling or in pain can be immense and at times unbearable. Over an extended period, such compassion can lead to emotional and physical exhaustion. This *compassion fatigue*, which sometimes affects even professional caregivers, may also result in insomnia, headaches, intestinal distress, irritability, anxiety, depression, helplessness, cynicism, confusion, isolation, and guilt (Figley 1997).

In addition, parents helping or caring for service members suffering from post-traumatic stress may experience *secondary traumatic stress*, in which a caregiver experiences post-traumatic stress symptoms that "mirror" those of the one who was traumatized. Symptoms of secondary traumatic stress include jumpiness, hypervigilance, an altered (either heightened or greatly diminished) sense of danger, images of traumatic experiences while awake, nightmares, social withdrawal, and mood swings (Stamm 1995).

Some of these symptoms, such as fatigue and anxiety, are considered a natural cost of caring otherwise known as *compassion stress* (Figley 1997). It's possible, though, to circumvent the more debilitating or prolonged problems associated with compassion fatigue that will interfere with your ability to care for and support your service member. For example, if your service member has a serious physical and/or psychological injury, we recommend that you adopt the mind-set of a marathon runner. In other words, envision the healing process as a long road with many ups and downs that requires a consistent, steady pace. If you were to run your fastest, giving it your all, you would collapse long before you reached the finish line. Even if your service member is struggling only with the common reintegration and/or practical issues we reviewed in chapters 1 and 2, it can be helpful to consider this as a marathon too and pace yourself as you support him or her on the path to readjustment.

Consider How You Cope

Almost a decade later I am still processing it all. Much like giving birth to him, this experience has made me a better person—stronger, with more compassion for others and for myself. (Susan)

The strain of supporting a son or daughter through readjustment naturally causes parents to seek ways to alleviate their stress.

Yet another common consequence of caring for an injured loved one is the tendency to lose sight of one's own needs and well-being. You may be tempted to rely on ineffective or unhealthy ways of coping with compassion stress. It's therefore highly important that you examine how you cope and take care of yourself by evaluating those strategies you already use—both healthy and unhealthy—and determining which, if any, need to be increased, decreased, or quit. Unhealthy coping strategies include overeating, smoking, drinking excessively, or using other substances to calm your nerves (see chapter 1). Temporarily, these behaviors may numb or dampen your distress, leading you to feel less emotional pain and giving you some relief from worrisome thoughts about your service member. However, over time they can interfere with your ability to provide your service member with the care and support he or she needs. One way to identify and monitor your current healthy and unhealthy coping strategies is to list them in a chart, such as below:

Healthy Coping Strategies	**How Often Used?**
1. *Jogging* 2. *Playing the guitar* 3. *Talking to a friend* 4. *Prayer and church* 5. *Volunteering as coach for Little League*	1. *About once a week* 2. *Twice this month* 3. *Once or twice a week* 4. *Usually every other Sunday* 5. *Felt too busy to commit any time to this season*
Unhealthy Coping Strategies	**How Often Used?**
1. *Drinking a bottle of wine* 2. *Eating a pint of ice cream* 3. *Staying in bed all day* 4. *Going on frivolous spending sprees*	1. *Nightly* 2. *Twice this month* 3. *Once a week* 4. *Once a month*

Once you've made your list, determine how to increase your use of those strategies that are healthy and add new strategies that may be more effective or doable. Think about what is keeping you from using healthy strategies on a more regular basis and develop a plan to overcome those barriers. For example, are you more likely to go on regular jogs if you have a friend join you and if you plan what days you will do this in advance? At the same time, consider how you might reduce your use of unhealthy strategies by replacing them with healthy ones. For example, rather than eating a pint of ice cream when you're feeling stressed, pick up the phone and call a trusted friend.

The goal is to have a wide range of strategies at your disposal to plug into a daily self-care regimen as well as to rely on during times of stress. Even if certain techniques you are currently using to manage stress are working quite well, we encourage you to supplement them with additional strategies from those furnished below.

How Do I Create a Self-Care Regimen?

> *I am very proud of what my daughter has accomplished and what she is currently doing. I see that she is happy with her current assignment. For me, I find that too much of my time is spent worrying about my daughter, and I need to spend my energies on other matters—like enjoying my life and not living for an answer to the most recent e-mail.* (Robert)

As we mentioned earlier, when running a marathon it's important to pace yourself, but you also must thoughtfully care for yourself along the way, taking breaks when necessary and reaching out for emotional support and encouragement. In this section we'll give you strategies and tools for establishing an effective self-care regimen to complement the healthy strategies you are already using.

Just Relax

If there's one thing that parents lack most, it's *time*. You may be raising school-age children, going to school yourself, working outside the home, or doing it all, in addition to caring for your returning service member and maintaining your home. But in order to keep all these balls in the air, it's essential that you find time to simply relax and refuel. The problem is that most people tend to think that taking time for themselves means setting aside a whole afternoon or weekend, when what people actually benefit from most is regular, brief intervals of relaxation.

The ideal way to maintain emotional and physical health as the busy parent of a reintegrating service member is to schedule brief relaxation periods each day. Try to schedule three 15-minute blocks, or one half hour and two 10-minute periods, for relaxation between the time you wake up and the time you go to bed. Think of these times as appointments you make with yourself. Try your best to keep these "me" appointments, but don't stress about them.

Create a Relaxation Menu

Once you have your "me" appointments scheduled, decide what type of relaxation you will use during those times. Create a "menu" of activities to choose from for your "me" appointments. Here are some options to consider:

- Read a leisure magazine or watch a favorite movie.
- Take a hike, a walk, or at least a short stroll.
- Use one of your favorite apps on your smart phone or tablet (e.g., solitaire, Sudoku).
- Enjoy a hobby like woodworking, photography, or model building.
- Practice yoga or meditation.

- Take a leisurely car or bike ride.
- Knit, paint, or just doodle.
- Dig in the garden or just sit in the sun.
- Take a hot shower or bath.
- Play or listen to music.

Write down your options and keep your relaxation menu where you can easily find it. Or better yet, use your smart phone or tablet to store your relaxation menu, as well as to remind you of your "me" appointments through the calendar function. Whatever you choose to do to relax, begin each activity by taking a deep breath and letting it out slowly as you think, *Relax*. Then enjoy your relaxation time—you deserve it! You may also want to refer to your relaxation menu whenever you find you have unexpected free time.

Slow Breathing

You may have noticed that when you get stressed, anxious, or overwhelmed, you breathe rapidly and shallowly. This type of breathing can lead to symptoms like dizziness, shaking, and loss of focus. In addition, the powerful interconnection between mind and body can cause rapid breathing to lead to increased anxiety, which in turn may lead to hyperventilation and eventually a panic attack. This is because rapid breathing sends a message to your mind that you are under threat, which then triggers a further increase in breathing rate as you become more anxious. A panic attack occurs when this feedback cycle culminates in a loss of physical and emotional control.

The good news is this mind-body connection can actually be harnessed to not only circumvent panic, but also lower your overall stress level and prevent future anxiety episodes. Just as rapid, shallow breathing sends your mind a message of threat, slow, controlled breathing sends a message of safety and calm. Here is a slow breathing technique that you can use to send yourself the message *Relax*.

Slow Breathing Exercise

1. Take a normal (not deep) breath in. Hold it while you count to five.

2. As you breathe out, say to yourself, *Relax*, in a calm, soothing manner.

3. Breathe in and out slowly through your nose in a six-second cycle, breathing in for three seconds and out for three seconds. This will produce a rate of ten breaths per minute. Every time you breathe out, tell yourself, *Relax*.

4. At the end of each minute (after ten breaths), hold your breath again for five seconds and then continue breathing using the six-second cycle.

If you have a smart phone or tablet, there are apps that can walk you through similar breathing exercises using a voice prompt.

To be most effective, this slow breathing exercise should be practiced for a minimum of five minutes several times per day whether you are feeling noticeably anxious or not. The great thing about this exercise is that you can do it just about anywhere, any time, without anybody else knowing. By regularly practicing the skill of slow breathing, you will not only find that it comes to you much more naturally and easily during times of high stress, but you will lower your overall anxiety level as well. Be sure to share this exercise with your service member and other loved ones—they all could benefit from some relaxation too.

Mind Your Body

Caring for someone with physical or mental health problems requires optimal physical health. Maintaining a strong and healthy body will make you better able to support your service member during the reintegration process. Here are some tips for minding your body.

Eat Well

It's common for people's eating habits to change during periods of stress. Anxiety, depression, physical pain, sleep disturbance, and medications can all affect a person's appetite and eating habits. Pay close attention to your eating habits when you are under stress. You may find that you are eating too little, too much, or simply too much of the wrong foods. Perhaps stress or fatigue has diminished your appetite, or conversely you may eat when you're feeling stressed or anxious, not because you're actually hungry. Perhaps your service member's erratic or unhealthy diet has affected your own eating habits. Try to stay on a regular meal schedule (if you have a reduced appetite, this may mean that you must push yourself to eat), and drink plenty of water throughout the day.

Stay Fit

Physical exercise is one of the most powerful yet simple and convenient strategies to care for your mind and body. Whatever type of activity you choose, regular exercise can not only improve your physical health but also lessen your stress and lift your mood. If you currently don't have an exercise routine, figure out how to make exercise or physical activity a regular part of your life. Start by selecting a type of exercise you enjoy and set realistic, small goals; when you meet a goal, reward yourself in a positive way—treat yourself to a small purchase or a visit to your favorite café, for example. You may want to join a club or team that is committed to preparing for a specific goal, like a run or bike ride to raise money for charity, maybe one that helps veterans or wounded service members.

Maintaining an exercise routine can be difficult when you're caring for or preoccupied with concerns about an injured or struggling service member. Regular walks or trips to the gym, for example, can be frequently disrupted by your loved one's physical or psychological needs. So make sure to always have a "plan B." That means if you have a plan to exercise with somebody, be prepared to go it alone; or if you need to stay close by your service member or near a phone, have an indoor exercise option at the ready. This could be an exercise video, a cardio machine, or something as low tech as running in place, climbing stairs, or jumping rope. Remember that when it comes to reducing your stress and improving your mood, cardio workouts are best, while strength training can help you accomplish the heavy lifting sometimes required of caregivers.

Get Good Sleep

[The impact of my son's deployment] has caused so much stress, sleepless nights. (Paul)

One of the most common struggles we hear about from parents of deployed service members is trouble sleeping. Maybe you developed poor sleep habits or even insomnia during your son's deployment as you lay awake worrying about his safety, and now that he's back, your sleep problems have only worsened as you toss and turn concerned about how about he is readjusting.

As we mentioned in chapter 1, it's also very common for service members to suffer sleep disturbances following deployment. If your service member has returned to live in your home, you may find yourself suffering right along with him or her as you provide company on sleepless nights or lie awake listening to the drone of the television. You may even find your sleep disrupted by your service member's mid-sleep screaming or thrashing.

As much as you want to be there for your son or daughter, try as much as possible to maintain a regular sleep schedule. This may mean going to bed even though your service member can't sleep, or resisting the urge to check on him or her during the night. You might consider wearing earplugs if you head to bed before your service member does, but don't hesitate to ask him or her to keep the noise to a minimum. Asking for nighttime courtesy does not mean that you are not sympathetic to your service member's sleep problems. Remember that if you are fatigued, you will be less able to help your service member heal.

Regardless of the cause, sleep problems can have negative consequences for both your physical and mental health. For this reason, it's critical that you identify any sleep challenges and then develop healthy strategies to address them. Below are some tips for healthy sleeping that both you and your service member can employ to improve your sleep and overall health.

- Stick to a routine sleep schedule as much as possible (go to bed and wake at the same time—even on weekends).
- Nap as little as possible during the day. If you need to nap, keep it to thirty minutes or less, and earlier in the day is better.
- Limit caffeine throughout the day, including coffee, black tea, energy drinks, sodas, and certain foods like chocolate.
- Exercise, but not close to bedtime.
- Establish a regular "wind down" routine before going to bed that includes relaxing activities.
- Don't drink alcohol or smoke to fall asleep.
- Take time to create a comfortable sleeping environment. (A night-light is okay, but otherwise keep it dark; make sure your bedding and room temperature are comfortable.)
- Before going to bed, remind yourself of a few positive things you made happen that day.
- If you are awake in bed, don't watch the clock. This only creates more anxiety about not sleeping.

You and your service member can further improve your sleep by using the following sleep strategies, which may seem counterintuitive but are quite beneficial (Perlis et al. 2008). *First*, if you don't fall asleep within fifteen minutes of going to bed, or if you awaken and can't return to sleep within fifteen minutes, get out of bed and go do something relaxing in another room until you get sleepy (read a book, do a light chore, do a crossword puzzle, listen to quiet music). Once you feel drowsy, get up and go back to bed. If once again you can't fall asleep within fifteen minutes, return to doing something relaxing in another room. Once sleepy, return to bed. Repeat as many times as needed.

Second, limit your activities in the bedroom to *sleep* and *sex*. No watching TV. No playing computer games. No surfing the Internet, listening to music, or talking on the phone. No paying bills. No worrying. No eating. No exercising or actively playing with your pet. In addition, make your bed the *only* place you sleep. Don't sleep on the couch, in an easy chair, or on the floor. When you combine this sleep practice with the one above, you are using a sleep strategy formally known as *stimulus control*. The underlying idea is to strengthen your mental association of your bed and bedroom with good sleep and to weaken your mental association of your bed and bedroom with wakefulness, activity, or frustration. In a nutshell, here's what you do:

1. Don't engage in any activities in your bedroom other than sleep and sex.
2. Go to bed with the intent of falling asleep.
3. If you don't fall asleep in fifteen minutes (or as soon as you're feeling annoyed by your wakefulness), get out of bed and go to another room and do something relaxing that you have pre-planned.
4. Once sleepy, go back to bed.
5. Repeat steps 3 and 4 as many times as needed until you fall asleep.
6. Get up at the same time every morning, seven days a week, no matter how much sleep you've gotten that night.

It can be very challenging for you and your service member to put these sleep habits into practice. Nonetheless, we encourage you both not to give up; it will take time and practice, but these positive strategies can indeed help.

Mind Your Mind

I worry more and am concerned for her. Just being a mother and the way moms are to their child.... Just be there for them, love them, and do a lot of praying. (Blanca)

While your service member was deployed, no doubt you were anxious and worried for his or her safety—maybe even on a daily basis or pretty much all the time. Now that your service member has returned, this worry doesn't just evaporate. Instead, you may find yourself worrying about your service member's reintegration into civilian life or how to support his or her recovery from physical or psychological injuries. You may feel sadness as you watch your service member struggle to fit in or adapt to a civilian job. As we discussed in chapter 4, if your service member suffered a debilitating or deforming injury, your sadness may turn to grief as you face the truth of what was lost. You may express this sadness or grief at times by crying, withdrawing from others or from activities you used to enjoy, or feeling more tired, less motivated, or less hopeful than usual.

When people feel anxious, worried, or depressed, they commonly experience unhelpful thoughts or images that further affect their emotions, actions, and even physical health. Even if your worries and sadness are understandable, you may wish that you were better able to manage and control your negative thoughts and feelings so that they no longer affected your sleep, activities, or relationships. While there may be times when you feel as if your worry or sadness has taken on a life of its own, there are actually practical ways that you can control these thoughts so that they don't control you.

Thought Control

Negative thought patterns can become so automatic that you don't even realize you're having them. Thus, in order to stop them, you must first identify those automatic thoughts, which may come in the form of negative self-talk (what you say to yourself) or negative images, and then increase your awareness of when you typically have them. One really good way to do this is to use a Thought/Image Record like the one below. This coping tool involves tracking the following information on a daily basis:

- What situation triggered my negative thoughts, self-talk, or images?
- What went through my mind during or after the situation? What were my automatic negative thoughts, self-talk, or images?
- How did I feel? What did I do? What were my reactions or behaviors?

Triggering Situation	Automatic Negative Thoughts, Self-Talk, or Images	Emotions, Reactions, or Behaviors
My son was just diagnosed with PTSD.	*It's my fault for letting him join the military.* *He'll never be able to work or go to college.* Images of him being poor and alone	Intense anxiety, guilt, and sadness Muscle tension, rapid heart rate, sleep problems Couldn't concentrate at work Canceled plans to go out to dinner with friend; refused to answer phone calls

By keeping a record like this, you'll discover how thoughts and images have tremendous power over your feelings and overall stress level. You'll also notice that although these negative thoughts and images may seem rational, they often represent the worst-case scenario. In other words, they often are worries about the most awful things that could happen, which in all probability *won't* happen. The good news is that once you identify these unhelpful automatic thoughts or images, you can intervene by challenging them, modifying them, or replacing them with positive messages. The goal is to make your thinking more realistic and productive. For example, you could replace the automatic negative thoughts above with positive self-talk like *My son is strong. I'm going to be strong too* or *He can get help for his PTSD and get better.* Similarly, you could replace the negative images with more positive ones, like your son's homecoming celebration or him proudly wearing his uniform. This thought monitoring and control technique can help you better manage your moods and stress level. You may want to share it with your service member too.

However, if you have tried using techniques like these and other coping strategies on your own and still find yourself in a low mood most of the time every day for longer than a week or two, and it's affecting your daily routine, it may be that your sadness has turned into something more serious like depression that requires professional help. If you are experiencing thoughts of suicide, it's imperative that you seek help immediately. The National Suicide Prevention Lifeline (1-800-273-8255) is one good place to start. See chapter 3 for a more in-depth discussion of depression and strategies to help.

Identifying and Restoring Challenged Beliefs

> *I married a Marine knowing full well what I was getting into. But never in a million years when I brought a helpless, innocent five-pound baby into this world did I expect to send him to war once, let alone seven times.* (Deborah)

In addition to tracking and challenging your negative thoughts, another useful exercise is to take time to reflect on your beliefs and how they may have shifted as a result of your service member's deployment. Having watched your son or daughter go through the ups and downs of the deployment cycle, you may find that you now have a few questions of your own. Maybe you're frustrated by the treatment your daughter has received from her superiors, her community, or even the VA system and are now questioning your own beliefs about your country and the military. On the other hand, you may have been against your son's enlistment but after seeing how he has matured and grown now feel more positively about the military.

Perhaps the stress of your daughter's deployment caused you to question your own strength and courage. Or maybe your son returned with physical or psychological injuries that have shaken you to the core and led you to question your worth as a parent. In any case it's important that you consider whether your beliefs may have shifted, and be sure to address any feelings of guilt or shame that may arise. Here is an exercise that will help you restore those beliefs that have been challenged.

Restoring Challenged Beliefs Exercise

Write down a belief you had prior to your service member's deployment(s) that was challenged, then the events or situations that challenged it. The goal is to integrate these challenges into your prior beliefs in the most adaptive, healthy way. This means rather than allowing the challenges to destroy your prior beliefs, find ways in which you can learn from these struggles and incorporate that learning to form new beliefs. Here's an example:

Prior Belief	Challenge	New Belief
I'm able to withstand stress.	I was overwhelmed with worry during my son's deployment.	*There are some stresses that are too much to bear on my own. If my son is deployed or under threat again, I'll seek out more support and use better strategies to manage my stress.*

Another way to restore your beliefs is to find meaning or benefit in the events that challenged them. Maybe your daughter's deployment gave you the opportunity to spend more time with your grandchildren. Or maybe you enjoyed taking care of your son's pet while he was away. It could be that you met other service members' parents who are now your close friends, or you may even have learned to use Facebook and other social networking sites that you wouldn't have otherwise tried. Make a list of all the things and people that have positively shaped your life because of your service member's deployment. You may even think of benefits that your service member has reaped, such as new friendships, improved self-discipline, or college funding.

Now that you're aware of the signs and symptoms of challenged beliefs, you may begin to see them in your service member as well, but even if you don't, feel free to talk with your service member about the impact of his or her deployment on you both. You might invite a discussion by saying something like **"While I have some idea about the things that you experienced during deployment, I would like to hear how your beliefs or views about yourself and the world may have been challenged or changed by your experience and maybe share how mine have been as well."** This sharing may be a process that requires several conversations to unfold. Don't be surprised if your service member shares something that shocks or even disappoints you. Be careful not to turn the discussion into a debate (e.g., about religion or patriotism), but feel free to point out if your service member's new beliefs seem unhealthy or unhelpful. He or she may even do the same for you! Finally, be sure to end your sharing on a positive note by talking about the benefits that you each have gained from the deployment experience. As you sit together and come to understand each other's experiences and views about these experiences, you're bound to feel a sense of reintegration and healing within your family.

Express Yourself

Although I know I'm not, I often feel that I am alone in coping with deployment. (Oscar)

Like your service member, you may be the "strong and silent type" or may believe that talking about your feelings and struggles equates to complaining. Maybe you feel as if you don't have the right to talk about your concerns for your service member when there are parents out there whose son or daughter never made it home. It's also easy during times like these to feel alone, as though no one can really understand what you're going through. But reaching out for support and expressing your thoughts and feelings are necessary aspects of self-care that will allow you in turn to better care for your service member. Here are some ways in which you can reach out and express yourself.

Talk to Someone You Trust

It can be extremely beneficial to share your feelings with someone you trust: your partner (e.g., spouse), a close friend or buddy, a therapist or counselor, a clergy member, or a family member. Although some people tend to avoid sharing their feelings, for various reasons—not wanting to burden others, feeling as if others won't understand, not wanting to appear needy, fearing how others will react—we recommend that you identify at least one person with whom you can talk. Be receptive to this person's support and care. Talking to a professional who won't judge you or be critical of your feelings, such as a therapist, counselor, spiritual advisor, or clergy, can also help.

Share the News

In addition to voicing your struggles and concerns, relating what your service member or his or her unit accomplished while deployed can foster a more positive attitude and improve your mood, as can sharing good news and stories of more recent successes. Let others in your neighborhood, workplace, or community know how proud you are of your son or daughter's military service. Show them a photo. Ask them to join you in contributing to the larger mission by sending care packages to those who are still deployed or by doing something to raise awareness about the positive aspects of military service. Sharing helps you feel better—it feels good to let others know that you support your military son or daughter, even if he or she is currently struggling. Yet remember that not everyone will be eager to hear about your service member. Therefore, be thoughtful about whom you choose to share with, and don't let someone's lack of excitement dampen your spirit.

Join a Parents' Group

> *If the first group—whether Blue Star Moms, Military Moms, etc.—[that you connect] with is not a good fit, keep exploring other organizations (there are many such organizations) until a good fit is found. The key for me was to get a bigger picture and to not only feel like I was supporting my son, but all of the troops who "had his back" and those who had served before him.* (Clara)

We've heard from many parents that talking with others who truly understand what they're going through or have been through is one of the best sources of support both during and after deployment. So joining (or starting) a group for parents of service members who have deployed can provide a sense of camaraderie and understanding. These connections can provide you with invaluable practical and emotional support. However, recognize that even within these groups, parents' experiences of deployment and reintegration can vary tremendously. If you are or were in the military yourself, you may want to reach out to people you know from your own service, since you share a common experience and understanding.

Journal

While talking to somebody you trust or joining a parents' organization can be incredibly helpful, journaling on a regular basis—whether daily, weekly, or whenever the mood strikes you; in a notebook or electronically—can also be a useful tool for expressing concerns and feelings about your son or daughter or whatever you're experiencing. We have heard that parents find the freedom to write about any aspect of their experience without risk of judgment by others very beneficial. We recommend the following guidelines if you choose to journal:

- Write about challenging as well as positive experiences.
- Write about events, but also the way they make you feel. Express what is in your heart.
- Go back and read your journal every few weeks or months to get some perspective on the patterns, themes, changes, and growth that you're experiencing.
- If you've never kept a journal before, don't give up if you forget to write in it or feel as if you don't have anything to say. Just write whatever or whenever you can without feeling pressure to do it perfectly.

You may find that journaling actually helps you improve your communication with your service member, especially if he or she isn't living with you. This form of expression may become your launching pad for writing e-mails or letters to your service member on a regular basis.

Monitor Yourself

Now that you've learned a variety of strategies to help you cope with your service member's reintegration challenges, it's time to start putting them into practice. But in order to successfully implement these strategies, you must first develop a means of monitoring your stress and your use of coping strategies.

Take Your Temperature

I'm still working on compassion fatigue. I'm better at saying "No, that doesn't work for me right now" or "Let me think on it and I'll get back to you." (Chase)

Many parents believe that their concerns should revolve around their service member. Others believe that acknowledging difficulties makes it more challenging to focus on their service member's needs. Yet tracking how you're doing on a regular basis will allow you to be a better champion for your service member in the long run.

This can be as easy as taking a five-minute break each day to ask yourself, *How am I doing?* You can simply rate your level of stress or distress on a scale from 0 (none) to 10 (extremely high) and record this information on your smart phone or calendar, in your notebook, or wherever is most convenient. It's similar to tracking your temperature over time. If your temperature remains in the normal range, then that's a good sign. A steady increase or spike in temperature (i.e., a fever) indicates that something is wrong—maybe you're getting sick and need to see a doctor or rest so you can fight off an infection. Not assessing how you're doing on a regular basis and ignoring small signs of physical or emotional stress may lead to bigger problems down the road. A quick daily assessment can help you determine when you need to increase your use of healthy coping strategies and reduce your use of any unhealthy ones.

Conclusion

As you reviewed the self-care strategies above, you may have identified several areas of your life that can be altered to improve your ability to cope and to support your service member both on a daily basis and in the long term. Again, remember that you are running a marathon, not a sprint. Be careful not to overwhelm yourself by trying to make too many changes at once. Begin with the areas with which you are most concerned, and stay focused on those areas before moving on to other issues. If you are suffering from insomnia, for instance, begin by focusing on improving your sleep, because doing so will give you more energy to invest in other self-care strategies. Also, remember to set reasonable expectations for yourself so that you can enjoy self-care success!

Chapter Tips

- You bring to the table many strengths and healthy ways of handling challenges. You've been through a lot. To remain healthy and resilient now that your service member has returned, *cope positively*. Care for yourself too!
- The more you're aware of how you're doing, the better able you will be to manage compassion stress and prevent compassion fatigue or secondary traumatic stress. Check your *emotional temperature* routinely.
- Staying physically fit—from getting good sleep to regularly exercising to following a healthy diet—will give you the stamina to best support your service member.
- Brief but regular periods of relaxation can help reduce your stress. Make time for relaxing activities and slow breathing exercises!
- Believe it or not, *self-talk*—what you say to yourself—plays a powerful role in how you feel and act. Begin to take more control of your thinking patterns.

- Express your thoughts and feelings to someone you trust, in an informal or formal parents' group, through writing, or by whatever means works best for you. Find outlets for support.

- Take the time to consider whether and how your beliefs have changed as a result of your service member's deployment. Be sure to reflect on the positive changes as well. Then sit down with your service member as well as other loved ones and share your thoughts and experiences. You may find this to be one of the most meaningful conversations you'll ever have with your family.

- For some suggested sources of further information and support, turn to the list of resources at the back of the book.

The Caregiver Support Program

In 2010 the Veterans Health Administration (VHA) implemented the Caregiver Support Program, which provides services to caregivers of anyone seriously injured during military service after September 11, 2001. If your veteran has injuries such as TBI and/or mental health disorders that significantly impair his or her daily functioning, you may be eligible for this program. Eligible caregivers may be provided with mental health counseling (but not prescription medications), education and training, other services, and a federal tax-free stipend. Caregivers can also receive travel reimbursement (including lodging when needed) for accompanying their veteran to medical appointments. Interested and eligible family members must attend and complete a VHA-sponsored Family Caregiver training. In order to determine eligibility, the caregiver and veteran will need to jointly fill out an application form (10-10CG). To obtain further information or to contact the Family Caregiver Support Coordinator for your area, visit www.caregiver.va.gov or call the Caregiver Support Line at 1-855-260-3274.

Resources

The following books, websites, and other resources can provide valuable information and support to service members and their families. Some of these resources are more for service members, while others are specifically for parents, caregivers, partners (e.g., spouses), or children of service members. Please note that while we are familiar with and can recommend many of these resources, we are not implicitly endorsing any resource by including it in the list. This list is not by any means all-inclusive, and some information may change following publication. Updated resources may be found on our website at www.courageafterfire.com/links.

Books

We have broken down the books and guides in this list into three categories, by author. First are books written by parents of service members; then, military spouses and laypersons; finally, mental health or medical professionals.

By Parents of Service Members

Faith of Our Sons: A Father's Wartime Diary by Frank Schaeffer (Carroll & Graf Publishers, 2004)

Keeping Faith: A Father-Son Story about Love and the United States Marine Corps by Frank Schaeffer and John Schaeffer (Carroll & Graf Publishers, 2002)

Our Sons, Our Daughters: A National Guard Parent's Guidebook to Deployment by Paula Sumrall (National Guard Family Program Office, 2007)

Your Soldier Your Army: A Parents' Guide by Vicki Cody (Association of the US Army, 2005)

By Military Spouses and Laypersons

The Complete Idiot's Guide to Life as a Military Spouse by Lissa McGrath (Alpha, 2008)

Confessions of a Military Wife by Mollie Gross (Savas Beatie, 2009)

A Family's Guide to the Military for Dummies by Sheryl Garrett and Sue Hoppin (John Wiley & Sons, 2009)

Heroes at Home: Help and Hope for America's Military Families by Ellie Kay (Bethany House, 2002)

Love Our Vets: Restoring Hope for Families of Veterans with PTSD by Welby O'Brien (Deep River Books, 2012)

Separated by Duty, United in Love: A Guide to Long-Distance Relationships for Military Couples by Shellie Vandevoorde (Citadel Press, 2006)

Surviving Deployment: A Guide for Military Families by Karen Pavlicin (Elva Resa Publishing, 2003)

By Mental Health or Medical Professionals

After the War Zone: A Practical Guide for Returning Troops and Their Families by Laurie Slone, PhD and Matthew Friedman, MD, PhD (Da Capo Press, 2008)

Back from the Front: Combat Trauma, Love, and the Family by Aphrodite Matsakis, PhD (Sidran Institute Press, 2007)

Counseling Military Families: What Mental Health Professionals Need to Know by Lynn Hall (Routledge, 2008)

Courage After Fire: Coping Strategies for Troops Returning from Iraq and Afghanistan and Their Families by Keith Armstrong, LCSW, Suzanne Best, PhD, and Paula Domenici, PhD (Ulysses Press, 2006)

Down Range: To Iraq and Back by Bridget Cantrell, PhD, and Chuck Dean (WordSmith Books, 2005)

Full Catastrophe Living: Using the Wisdom of Your Body and Mind to Face Stress, Pain, and Illness by Jon Kabat-Zinn, PhD (Bantam Dell, 1990)

Mindfulness Meditation for Pain Relief: Guided Practices for Reclaiming Your Body and Your Life by Jon Kabat-Zinn, PhD (Sounds True, Inc., 2009)

Once a Warrior—Always a Warrior: Navigating the Transition from Combat to Home—Including Combat Stress, PTSD, and mTBI by Charles W. Hoge, MD (GPP Life, 2010)

Hotlines, Crisis Lines, and Complaint Lines

(All numbers are toll free.)

Benefiting Veterans Support Hotline (includes support for military sexual trauma)

1-888-4VETS25 (483-8725)

Caregiver Support Line

1-855-260-3274

Defense Centers of Excellence for Psychological Health and Traumatic Brain Injury 24/7 Outreach Center

1-866-966-1020

The Joint Commission's Complaint Hotline

1-800-994-6610 (or e-mail complaint@jointcommission.org)

Military OneSource 24/7 Hotline

1-800-342-9647

National Coalition for Homeless Veterans Crisis Line

1-877-424-3838

National Suicide Prevention Lifeline

1-800-273-TALK (8255) (This lifeline is for anyone struggling with concerns about harming themselves; veterans, service members, or anyone concerned about a veteran or service member should press "1" for the Veterans Crisis Line—see below.)

National Veterans Foundation Live Help Line

1-888-777-4443 (or chat online at chat.nvf.org/chat.php)

Red Cross Military Family Hotline

1-877-272-7337

US Department of Veterans Affairs (VA)

Office of Inspector General Complaint Hotline

1-800-488-8244 (or e-mail vaoighotline@va.gov)

Vet Center Combat Call Center

1-877-WAR-VETS (927-8387)

Veterans Crisis Line

1-800-273-TALK (8255), press "1" (or chat online at veteranscrisisline.net or text to 838255)

Websites

Though the following list makes use of headings to note primary intended audience, topic, or format, many of these resources belong to more than one category. For reasons of space, however, we decided that each resource should appear only once. Therefore, be sure to skim all the categories to find the resources that may interest or be useful to you and your family.

Children of Service Members

Military Child Education Coalition

www.militarychild.org

Military Youth on the Move

apps.militaryonesource.mil/pls/psgprod/f?p=123:HOME2:0

Our Military Kids

www.ourmilitarykids.org

Traumatic Brain Injury: The Journey Home

"Helping Your Children Cope"

www.traumaticbraininjuryatoz.org/Caregivers-Journey/Session-Four/Helping-Your-Children-Cope.aspx

US Department of Veterans Affairs (VA) National Center for PTSD

"Children Coping with Deployment"

www.ptsd.va.gov/public/pages/children-coping-deployment.asp

"Web Links: Children and Teens"

www.ptsd.va.gov/public/web-resources/web-children-adolescents.asp

Employment

America's Heroes at Work

www.americasheroesatwork.gov

Farmer Veteran Coalition

www.farmvetco.org

Feds Hire Vets

www.fedshirevets.gov

Helmets to Hardhats

helmetstohardhats.org

Hire a Hero

hireahero.org

Hire America's Heroes

hireamericasheroes.org

Hire Heroes USA

www.hireheroesusa.org

Hire Veterans

www.hireveterans.com

Military.com

"Veteran Jobs"

www.military.com/veteran-jobs

Military Exits

www.militaryexits.com

Military Resume Writers

www.militaryresumewriters.com

My Next Move for Veterans

www.mynextmove.org/vets

National Resource Directory

"Veterans Job Bank"

www.nrd.gov/jobSearch/index

National Veterans' Training Institute

www.nvti.ucdenver.edu

Quintessential Careers

"Job Transitioning for Vets and Former Military"

www.quintcareers.com/former_military.html

Troops to Teachers

proudtoserveagain.com

USA.gov: The U.S. Government's Official Web Portal

www.usa.gov

US Department of Labor

"Veterans' Employment and Training Service (VETS)"

www.dol.gov/vets

US Department of Veterans Affairs (VA)

Veterans Employment Toolkit

va.gov/vetsinworkplace/index.asp

VA for Vets

(VA careers for veterans)

vaforvets.va.gov (*Resume Building Guide* available at http://vaforvets.va.gov/veterans/resources/Documents/Resume_Building_Guide_01062012.pdf)

Veterans Opportunity to Work (VOW) to Hire Heroes Act 2011

benefits.va.gov/VOW

VetSuccess

vetsuccess.gov

Veteranscorp: Helping Veterans Collaborate for Success

www.veteranscorp.org

Veterans Green Jobs

veteransgreenjobs.org

Walmart Jobs for Veterans and Transitioning Military

walmartcareerswithamission.com

Families of Service Members

Afterdeployment.org: Wellness Resources for the Military Community

www.afterdeployment.org

American Military Family (AMF)

www.amf100.org

Army Reserve Family Programs

arfp.org

Articles, Research, & Resources in Psychology

"Resources for Troops and Veterans, Their Families, and Those Who Provide Services to Them"

kspope.com/torvic/war.php

Corporation for National & Community Service: United We Serve

www.serve.gov

Defense Centers of Excellence for Psychological Health and Traumatic Brain Injury

www.dcoe.health.mil

Family and Friends for Freedom Fund

injuredmarinesfund.org

FOCUS: Family Resiliency Training for Military Families

focusproject.org

Google for Veterans and Families

www.googleforveterans.com

Homefront America: Supporting Military Families

homefrontamerica.org

The Joint Services Support System

"Yellow Ribbon Reintegration Program"

www.jointservicessupport.org/YRRP (Click "Change" at the top of the webpage if the default state and role it identifies for you are incorrect.)

Love Our Vets (PTSD Family Support)

www.loveourvets.org

Military Families United

militaryfamiliesunited.org

Military Family Link: Family Resilience and Cohesion

militaryfamilylink.com

Military Family Network

emilitary.org

Military Family Support

militaryfamilysupport.org

Military Family Support Center

milfamily.org

Military OneSource

www.militaryonesource.mil

M-SPAN: Military Support Programs and Networks for Our Service Members, Veterans, and Their Families

m-span.org

National Alliance on Mental Illness

nami.org

National Military Family Association

www.militaryfamily.org

Purple Star Veterans and Families: Strengthening the Homecoming Safety Net

purplestarfamilies.org

Real Warriors Campaign

realwarriors.net

Red Cross

"Supporting America's Military Families"

www.redcross.org/what-we-do/support-military-families

TRICARE

tricare.mil

US Department of Veterans Affairs (VA)

Caregiver Support

www.caregiver.va.gov

Center for Minority Veterans

va.gov/centerforminorityveterans

Center for Women Veterans

va.gov/womenvet

USA 4 Military Families

www.usa4militaryfamilies.dod.mil

USO

"USO Warrior and Family Care"

www.uso.org/warriorandfamilycare

Veteran CareGiver

veterancaregiver.com

Veterans' Families United Foundation

veteransfamiliesunited.org

Welcome Home Warrior: Serving Active Duty Veterans and Their Families

whwarrior.org

Financial Assistance

Allied Business Schools: Education 4 Military

education4military.com

The DKF Veterans Assistance Foundation

(Scholarships for OEF/OIF/OND veterans)

dkfveterans.com

US Department of Veterans Affairs (VA)

"Benefits of the Yellow Ribbon Program"

gibill.va.gov/benefits/post_911_gibill/yellow_ribbon_program.html

The GI Bill Web Site

gibill.va.gov

Health Care

Free Mental Health Services for Families of OEF/OIF/OND Service Members, Including Parents

The Coming Home Project

(For veterans and their families in the San Francisco Bay Area)

cominghomeproject.net

Give an Hour

(Check for services in your area)

giveanhour.org

Returning Veterans Project

(For veterans and their families in Oregon and southwest Washington)

returningveterans.com

SOFAR: Strategic Outreach to Families of All Reservists

(Check for services in your area)

sofarusa.org

The Soldiers Project

(Check for services in your area)

www.thesoldiersproject.org

General Benefits

Military.com

"Military Benefits"

(Includes veteran and survivor benefit information)

www.military.com/benefits

US Department of Veterans Affairs (VA)

"Benefits Fact Sheets"

www.vba.va.gov/vba/benefits/factsheets

"Federal Benefits for Veterans, Dependents and Survivors"

www.va.gov/opa/publications/benefits_book.asp

"Returning Servicemembers (OEF/OIF/OND)"

www.va.gov/healthbenefits/apply/returning_servicemembers.asp

USA.gov: eBenefits

www.ebenefits.va.gov

Veterans Benefits Administration

www.vba.va.gov/VBA

General Veterans' Health Issues

Air Compassion for Veterans (ACV)

aircompassionforveterans.org

Hooah 4 Health

hooah4usa.com

The Joint Commission

www.jointcommission.org

US Department of Defense (DoD) Military Health System

"MHS for Service Members, Retirees and Families"

health.mil/MHSFor/ServiceMembersandFamilies.aspx

US Department of Veterans Affairs (VA)

"Health Care"

www.va.gov/health

Office of Inspector General

www.va.gov/oig

"Returning Service Members (OEF/OIF/OND)"

www.oefoif.va.gov

War Related Illness and Injury Study Center (WRIISC)

www.warrelatedillness.va.gov

Military Sexual Trauma

Make the Connection

"Effects of Military Sexual Trauma"

maketheconnection.net/conditions/military-sexual-trauma

MilitarySexualTrauma.org

militarysexualtrauma.org

National Public Radio

"Military Sexual Trauma: A Little-Known Veteran Issue" (podcast)

www.npr.org/templates/story/story.php?storyId=126783956

NOW on PBS

"Military Sexual Trauma" (video)

www.pbs.org/now/shows/336/

US Department of Veterans Affairs (VA)

"Military Sexual Trauma"

www.mentalhealth.va.gov/msthome.asp

National Center for PTSD

"Military Sexual Trauma"

http.ptsd.va.gov/public/pages/military-sexual-trauma-general.asp

Online Health Management Platform

US Department of Veterans Affairs (VA)

My Health*e*Vet

www.myhealth.va.gov

Physical Health (for Traumatic Brain Injury, see below)

Afterdeployment.org: Wellness Resources for the Military Community

"Page 4—physical-injury"

www.afterdeployment.org/sites/default/files/library/physical-injury/files/assets/seo/page4.html

American Chronic Pain Association

theacpa.org

American Tinnitus Association

www.ata.org

Amputee Coalition

amputee-coalition.org

Blinded Veterans Association

bva.org

The Given Limb Foundation

www.givenlimb.org

Partners Against Pain

partnersagainstpain.com

US Department of Veterans Affairs (VA)

Center of Excellence for Limb Loss Prevention and Prosthetic Engineering

www.amputation.research.va.gov

"New Treatment Options for Tinnitus Sufferers"

www.va.gov/health/NewsFeatures/20110524a.asp

Polytrauma System of Care

www.polytrauma.va.gov

"VHA Pain Management"

www.va.gov/painmanagement

Veterans in Pain

vetsinpain.org

Post-Traumatic Stress

Dr. David Baldwin's Trauma Information Pages

www.trauma-pages.com

Gift from Within: PTSD Resources for Survivors and Caregivers

"Military Family Resources"

giftfromwithin.org/html/military-family-resources.html

International Society for Traumatic Stress Studies (ISTSS)

istss.org

PTSD Coach App

www.ptsd.va.gov/public/pages/PTSDCoach.asp

US Department of Veterans Affairs (VA) National Center for PTSD

www.ptsd.va.gov

Substance Abuse

National Institute on Drug Abuse

"Topics in Brief: Substance Abuse among the Military, Veterans, and Their Families"

www.drugabuse.gov/publications/topics-in-brief/substance-abuse-among-military-veterans-their-families

Substance Abuse and Mental Health Services Administration (SAMHSA)

"Military Families"

www.samhsa.gov/militaryfamilies

US Department of Veterans Affairs (VA)

"Summary of VA Treatment Programs for Substance Use Problems" www.mentalhealth.va.gov/res-vatreatmentprograms.asp

Suicide Prevention

National Suicide Prevention Lifeline

www.suicidepreventionlifeline.org

US Department of Veterans Affairs (VA)

"Suicide Prevention"

www.mentalhealth.va.gov/suicide_prevention/index.asp

Traumatic Brain Injury (TBI)

American Veterans with Brain Injuries (AVBI)

avbi.org

Brain Injury Association of America

www.biausa.org

Defense and Veterans Brain Injury Center

www.dvbic.org

TBI website

www.whatistbi.org

Traumatic Brain Injury: The Journey Home

(Site includes FAQ, resources for caregivers, and resources for families)

www.traumaticbraininjuryatoz.org

Veterans' Health Care Centers

US Department of Veterans Affairs (VA)

Vet Center

www.vetcenter.va.gov

"Where Do I Get the Care I Need?"

www.va.gov/health/findcare.asp

Higher Education

American Council on Education

"Military Students and Veterans"

www.acenet.edu/higher-education/Pages/Military-Students-and-Veterans.aspx

BigFuture: College Board

bigfuture.collegeboard.org

First Command Educational Foundation

www.fcef.com

The Jed Foundation

jedfoundation.org/professionals/programs-and-research/helping-our-student-veterans-succeed

Operation Vets

operationvets.com

Student Veterans of America

www.studentveterans.org

Today's GI Bill

www.todaysgibill.org

Homelessness

National Alliance to End Homelessness

"Veterans"

www.endhomelessness.org/section/issues/veterans

National Coalition for Homeless Veterans
nchv.org

National Coalition for the Homeless
Homeless Veterans Fact Sheet (PDF)
nationalhomeless.org/factsheets/veterans.pdf

US Department of Veterans Affairs (VA)
"Homeless Veterans"
www.va.gov/HOMELESS/index.asp

Parents of Service Members

Blue Star Mothers of America
www.bluestarmothers.org

Fathers of the Brave
fathersofthebrave.com

MarineParents.com
marineparents.com

Military Moms
militarymoms.net

Proud Army Moms
www.nammas.org/group/proudarmymoms

Parents of Service Members (Deceased)

American Gold Star Mothers
goldstarmoms.com

Bereaved Parents of the USA

bereavedparentsusa.org

Gold Star Dads of America

goldstardads.org

Service Members and Their Family Members/Caregivers

Advocacy and Community-Based Organizations

The American Legion

www.legion.org

American Veterans (AMVETS)

www.amvets.org

Challenge America

challengeamerica.com

Disabled American Veterans

dav.org

HadIt.com Veteran to Veteran

www.hadit.com

Iraq and Afghanistan Veterans of America (IAVA)

iava.org

National Association of American Veterans

naavets.org

National Association of County Veterans Service Officers

www.nacvso.org

National Veterans Foundation

nvf.org

National Veterans Legal Services Program

nvlsp.org

Real Warriors Campaign

realwarriors.net

ReMIND: The Bob Woodruff Foundation

remind.org

Swords to Plowshares

swords-to-plowshares.org

TAA (Transition Assistance Advisors) Program

www.taapmo.com

TurboTAP (Transition Assistance Program)

turbotap.org

US Soldiers Foundation

ussoldiersfoundation.org

US Welcome Home Foundation

uswelcomehome.org

Veterans of Foreign Wars

vfw.org

The Veterans' Voice

www.theveteransvoice.com

Blogs

Healing Combat Trauma

healingcombattrauma.com

Kyle Maynard's blog

kyle-maynard.com/blog

Milblogging.com: The World's Largest Index of Military Blogs (Milblogs)

milblogging.com

VA Benefit Blog: The Latest News on Your VA Benefits

www.vabenefitblog.com

VAntage Point: Dispatches from the U.S. Department of Veterans Affairs

www.blogs.va.gov

Podcasts

National Public Radio

The Impact of War Project (podcasts & articles)

www.npr.org/series/101336726/the-impact-of-war-project

The New Veteran (podcasts & articles)

www.npr.org/series/126742716/the-new-veteran

Social Networking Sites

Make the Connection

(Social networking platform for veterans)

maketheconnection.net

Veteran.com

(Online community for US veterans)

veteran.com

Veterans Health Administration (VHA)

www.facebook.com/VeteransHealth

twitter.com/veteranshealth

Wounded Warriors and Their Families

Air Force Wounded Warrior

www.woundedwarrior.af.mil

Azalea Charities

azaleacharities.org

Building Homes for Heroes

buildinghomesforheroes.org

Career Center for Wounded Warriors and Disabled Veterans

www.military.com/support

Impact a Hero

impactahero.org

Intrepid Fallen Heroes Fund

fallenheroesfund.org

Life Quest: Transitions

www.mylq.org

M1 for Vets

(Adaptive marksmanship program)

m1forvets.com

Northrop Grumman Careers: Operation IMPACT (Injured Military Pursuing Assisted Career Transition)

careers.northropgrumman.com/operation_impact.html

Operation Second Chance

operationsecondchance.org

Paralyzed Veterans of America

www.pva.org

Rebuild Hope

rebuildhope.org

Return to Work (R2W)

www.return2work.org

Semper Fi Fund

semperfifund.org

US Wounded Soldiers Foundation

uswoundedsoldiers.com

Vacations for Veterans

vacationsforveterans.org

Wounded Heroes Foundation

www.woundedheroesfund.net

References

Alexander, M. 1995. "Mild Traumatic Brain Injury: Pathophysiology, Natural History, and Clinical Management." *Neurology* 45: 1253–60.

American Chronic Pain Association (ACPA). 2012a. *ACPA Resource Guide to Chronic Pain Medication and Treatment.* http://theacpa.org/uploads/ACPA_Resource_Guide_2012_Update%20031912.pdf.

———. 2012b. "Pain Management Programs." http://www.theacpa.org/Pain-Management-Programs.

American Tinnitus Association (ATA). 2012a. "About Tinnitus." http://www.ata.org/for-patients/about-tinnitus.

———. 2012b. "ATA's Top Ten Most Frequently Asked Questions." http://www.ata.org/for-patients/faqs.

———. 2012c. "Management Tips." http://www.ata.org/for-patients/tips.

———. 2012d. "Support for Vets: One of Our Top Priorities." http://www.ata.org/action-alliance/support-for-veterans.

———. 2012e. "Treatment Information." http://www.ata.org/for-patients/treatment.

Baum, J. N.d. *Primary Care Issues in the OIF/OEF Veteran.* VA NWIHCS-Lincoln, NE. http://dhhs.ne.gov/behavioral_health/Documents/Baum-PrimaryCarc.pdf.

Bowlby, J. 1988. *A Secure Base: Parent-Child Attachment and Healthy Human Development.* London: Routledge.

Bureau of Labor Statistics (BLS), US Department of Labor. 2012. "Employment Situation of Veterans Summary." Economic News Release, March 20. http://www.bls.gov/news.release/vet.nr0.htm.

Center for Deployment Psychology. 2010. The Fundamentals of Traumatic Brain Injury (TBI) (online course). http://deploymentpsych.org/training/training-catalog/course-119-online-the-fundamentals-of-traumatic-brain-injury-tbi.

Centers for Disease Control and Prevention (CDC). 2012. "Severe Traumatic Brain Injury." http://www.cdc.gov/TraumaticBrainInjury/severe.html.

Defense and Veterans Brain Injury Center (DVBIC). 2012a. "Blast Injuries." http://www.dvbic.org/blast-injuries.

———. 2012b. "DoD Worldwide Numbers for TBI." http://www.dvbic.org/dod-worldwide-numbers-tbi.

———. 2012c. "TBI Basics." http://www.dvbic.org/tbi-basics.

Defense and Veterans Brain Injury Center (DVBIC) Working Group. 2008. "Acute Management of Mild Traumatic Brain Injury in Military Operational Settings." BrainLineMilitary.org. www.brainlinemilitary.org/content/2008/07/acute-management-mild-traumatic-brain-injury-military-operational-settings-clinical-practice.html.

Defense Medical Surveillance System (DMSS), Theater Medical Data Store (TMDS). 2012. "DoD Numbers for Traumatic Brain Injury Worldwide." http://www.dvbic.org/sites/default/files/uploads/dod-tbi-2000-2012.pdf.

Dobscha, S. K., R. Campbell, B. J. Morasco, M. Freeman, and M. Helfand. 2008. *Pain in Patients with Polytrauma: A Systematic Review.* Washington, DC: Department of Veterans Affairs. http://www.hsrd.research.va.gov/publications/esp/polytrauma.cfm.

Faul, M., L. Xu, M. Wald, and V. Coronado. 2010. *Traumatic Brain Injury in the United States: Emergency Department Visits, Hospitalizations, and Deaths 2002–2006.* Atlanta: US Department of Health and Human Services, Centers for Disease Control and Prevention, National Center for Injury Prevention and Control. http://www.cdc.gov/traumaticbraininjury/pdf/blue_book.pdf.

Figley, C. 1997. *Burnout in Families: The Systemic Costs of Caring.* Boca Raton, FL: CRC Press.

Giles, D. 2012. "Tinnitus Causes: How to Understand Military Tinnitus." EzineArticles.com. http://ezinearticles.com/?Tinnitus-Causes---How-to-Understand-Military-Tinnitusid=2265021.

Henry, J., T. Zaugg, P. Myers, C. Kendall, and M. Turbin. 2009. "Principles and Application of Educational Counseling Used in Progressive Audiologic Tinnitus Management." *Noise & Health,* Jan-Mar, 11(42): 33–48.

Hoge, C.W.; Castro, C.A.; Eaton, K.M. (2006) Impact of Combat Duty in Iraq and Afghanistan on Family Functioning: Findings from the Walter Reed Army Institute of Research Land Combat Study. In Human Dimensions in Military Operations – Military Leaders' Strategies for Addressing Stress and Psychological Support (pp. 5-1 – 5-6). Meeting Proceedings RTO-MP-HFM-134, Paper 5. Neuilly-sur-Seine, France: RTO.

Hoge, C., D. McGurk, J. Thomas, A. Cox, C. Engel, and C. Castro. 2008. "Mild Traumatic Brain Injury in US Soldiers Returning from Iraq." *New England Journal of Medicine* 358: 453–63.

Janoff-Bulman, R. 2002. *Shattered Assumptions: Towards a New Psychology of Trauma.* New York: Free Press.

Johnson, S. 2004. *The Practice of Emotionally Focused Couple Therapy: Creating Connection.* 2nd ed. New York: Brunner-Routledge.

Kushner, D. 1998. "Mild Traumatic Brain Injury: Toward Understanding Manifestations and Treatment." *Archives of Internal Medicine* 158: 1617–24.

Mayes, J. 2010. *Tinnitus Treatment Toolbox: A Guide for People with Ear Noise.* Victoria, BC, Canada: Trafford Publishing.

Military Child Education Coalition (MCEC). 2012. "Living in the New Normal (LINN)." http://www.militarychild.org/professionals/programs/living-in-the-new-normal-linn.

Minuchin, S. 1974. *Families and Family Therapy.* Cambridge, MA: Harvard University Press.

Nash, W. 2007. "Combat/Operational Stress Adaptations and Injuries." In *Combat Stress Injury: Theory, Research, and Management,* edited by C. Figley and W. Nash. New York: Routledge Taylor & Francis Group.

Perlis, M., C. Jungquist, M. Smith, and D. Posner. 2008. *Cognitive Behavioral Treatment of Insomnia: A Session-by-Session Guide.* New York: Springer.

President & Fellows of Harvard College. 2000–2006. "12 Things You Should Know about Pain Relievers." http://www.health.harvard.edu/fhg/updates/12-things-you-should-know-about-pain-relievers.shtml.

Radford, A., and MPR Associates, Inc. 2009. *Military Service Members and Veterans in Higher Education: What the New GI Bill May Mean for Postsecondary Institutions.* Washington, DC: American Council on Education.

Spelman, J., S. Hunt, K. Seal, and A. Burgo-Black. 2012. "Post Deployment Care for Returning Combat Veterans." *Journal of General Internal Medicine* 27: 1200–1209. doi:10.1007/sl1606-012-2061-1.

Stamm, B., ed. 1995. *Secondary Traumatic Stress: Self-Care Issues for Clinicians, Researchers, and Educators.* Lutherville, MD: Sidran Press.

"Troops with Tinnitus Could Find Relief." 2012. *Military Medical & Veterans Affairs Forum (M2VA)* 16(5) (August): 15.

US Department of Labor (DOL). 2012. *Good Jobs for Vets* (pamphlet).

US Department of Veterans Affairs, Department of Defense (VA/DoD). 2009. *Clinical Practice Guideline for Management of Concussion/mTBI.* Prepared by the Management of Concussion/mTBI Working Group with Support from The Office of Quality Performance, VA, Washington, DC & Quality Management Directorate, United States Army MEDCOM, Version 1.0.

Paula Domenici, PhD, is a counseling psychologist focused on deploymentrelated mental health issues with a specialization in post-traumatic stress disorder (PTSD). She has worked extensively with veterans, as well as educating clinicians who care for them. She currently trains military and civilian mental health providers across the country on evidencebased therapies and culturalsensitive practices for assisting the military community. Previously, she served as an American Psychological Association (APA) policy fellow in former Senator Clinton's office addressing concerns of veterans and seniors. Earlier, Domenici was a staff psychologist on the San Francisco Veteran's Administration's PTSD Clinical Team, treating veterans with combat trauma and supporting their spouses. She lives in Washington, DC.

Suzanne Best, PhD, is a clinical psychologist specializing in the study, evaluation, and treatment of PTSD and other traumarelated conditions. In her overten years with the PTSD Research Program at the San Francisco VA Medical Center, she directed numerous federally funded studies of combat veterans and law enforcement professionals with a focus on treatment development. She currently resides in Portland, OR, where she treats veterans, first responders, and civilian trauma survivors. In addition, she serves as an adjunct professor at Lewis and Clark Graduate School of Education and Counseling where she teaches courses in trauma psychology and is currently conducting a study of parents of Iraq and Afghanistan veterans.

Keith Armstrong, LCSW, is a clinical professor of psychiatry at the University of California, San Francisco. He is director of the San Francisco Veterans Administration's (SFVA) Family Therapy Program and the City College of San Francisco Veterans Outreach Program, and is a member of the SFVA's PTSD Clinical Team. In addition, he is a consultant for the Intensive Family Therapy program at the University of California, San Francisco. Armstrong has authored numerous clinical and research articles and chapters addressing the treatment of traumatized individuals and families. He is also a reviewer for the Journal of Traumatic Stress, a top journal in the field of traumatology, and he has conducted numerous radio, newspaper, and podcast interviews on the psychological treatment of veterans and families. He lives with his wife and two children in the San Francisco Bay Area.

FROM OUR PUBLISHER—

As the publisher at New Harbinger and a clinical psychologist since 1978, I know that emotional problems are best helped with evidence-based therapies. These are the treatments derived from scientific research (randomized controlled trials) that show what works. Whether these treatments are delivered by trained clinicians or found in a self-help book, they are designed to provide you with proven strategies to overcome your problem.

Therapies that aren't evidence-based—whether offered by clinicians or in books—are much less likely to help. In fact, therapies that aren't guided by science may not help you at all. That's why this New Harbinger book is based on scientific evidence that the treatment can relieve emotional pain.

This is important: if this book isn't enough, and you need the help of a skilled therapist, use the following resources to find a clinician trained in the evidence-based protocols appropriate for your problem. And if you need more support—a community that understands what you're going through and can show you ways to cope—resources for that are provided below, as well.

Real help is available for the problems you have been struggling with. The skills you can learn from evidence-based therapies will change your life.

Matthew McKay, PhD
Publisher, New Harbinger Publications

If you need a therapist, the following organization can help you find a therapist trained in cognitive behavioral therapy (CBT).

The Association for Behavioral & Cognitive Therapies (ABCT) Find-a-Therapist service offers a list of therapists schooled in CBT techniques. Therapists listed are licensed professionals who have met the membership requirements of ABCT and who have chosen to appear in the directory.

Please visit www.abct.org and click on *Find a Therapist*.

For additional support for patients, family, and friends, please contact the following:

National Center for PTSD
visit www.ptsd.va.gov